SUCH STUFF AS DREAMS

"We are such stuff as dreams are made on
And our little life is rounded with a sleep."
~ William Shakespeare, *The Tempest*

"O God, I could be bounded in a nutshell,
and count myself a king of infinite space,
were it not that I have bad dreams."
~ William Shakespeare, *Hamlet*

SUCH STUFF AS DREAMS

BY
EUGENE J. MAHON, MD

IPBOOKS.net
International Psychoanalytic Books

International Psychoanalytic Books (IPBooks)
New York • http://www.IPBooks.net

Such Stuff as Dreams

Published by IPBooks, Queens, NY
Online at: www.IPBooks.net

ISBN: 978-1-956864-00-7

For Delia, of course
and for Eugene, John and Emer

ABOUT THE AUTHOR

EUGENE MAHON MD is a Training and Supervising Psychoanalyst on the faculty of Columbia University Psychoanalytic Center for Training and Research. He is also a member of the Center for Advanced Psychoanalytic studies, Princeton, New Jersey. He was awarded the Alexander Beller Award by the Columbia Psychoanalytic Center in 1984. He has published many articles on a variety of topics such as A Longitudinal Study of Dreams, Screen Memories, Mourning, Dreaming and the Discovery of the Oedipus complex, Play and Working Through, Repression, Prejudice, Insight, The Golden Section; he has published applied psychoanalytic articles on Shakespeare, Sophocles, Samuel Beckett, Oscar Wilde, Samuel Taylor Coleridge; an article on Poetry and Psychoanalysis, as well as a volume of poetry and several plays on psychoanalytic topics. He is the author of three books: *A Psychoanalytic Odyssey*; *Rensal the Redbit* (a psychoanalytic fairy tale, translated into Italian) and *Boneshop of the Heart*. He practices Child Psychoanalysis and Adult Psychoanalysis in New York City.

Acknowledgements

I want to thank all the teachers and colleagues who have influenced my development as a psychoanalyst over the years: I am indebted to all of them. My first great indebtedness is to Delia Battin who has influenced all of my thinking, read and critiqued all of my publications and been an extraordinary ally, friend, colleague and spouse for half a century.

I have had great teachers throughout my psychoanalytic education at Columbia University Center for Psychoanalytic Training and Research and I would like to thank all of them, living and deceased: S.L.Feder; Lionel Ovesey, John A. Sours, Richard Druss, Peter Neubauer, Peter Blos, Marianne Kris, Lauretta Bender, Helen Meyers, Donald Meyers, Alexander Beller, Grace Abbate. Margaret Mahler, Robert Michels, Charles Sarnoff, Alberta Szalita, Eleanor Galenson, John Weber, Milton Viederman.

I would also like to thank all of my colleagues, deceased and living at the Center for Advanced Psychoanalytic Studies Princeton NJ: Richard Isay, Robert Kabcennel, Marianne Goldberger, Naomi Ragins, Tom Pappadis. John Howie, Jim Robinson, Monique King, Barbara Fajardo, Lester Schwartz, Robert Rodman, Jim Robinson, Barry Opatow, Alan Zients, Ana Maria Rizutto, Henry Smith, Sam Hoch, Roger Eddy, Richard Weiss, David Hurst, David Stevens, Stephen Silk, Mojgan Khademi, Beth Seelig, Sandra Park, Mary Margaret McClure, Philip Freeman, Stacy Keller.

I am indebted to my colleague, friend, psychoanalyst and artist David Hurst for the whimsical evocation of the Wolfman's dream, which he has entitled "WOLF DREAMS"

FOREWORD

by Theodore Jacobs, M.D.

Dreams have always been at the center of the analytic endeavor.
By his own estimation and those of analysts world-wide, Sigmund
Freud's most important contribution to psychoanalysis was his 1900
masterwork, *The Interpretation of Dreams*.

This seminal study, remarkable for Freud's capacity for self-analysis as
well as his illumination of the workings of the unconscious as it produces
its nightly creations, has been for more than a century, the fundamental
text and source for our understanding of the fascinating and enigmatic
world of dreams.

Our contemporary focus on other aspects of psychoanalysis; infant-
mother research, neuro-analysis, gender studies, the psychoanalytic
understanding of social and economic issues, and the ongoing discussions
and debates over competitive theoretical approaches, has largely replaced
interest in dreams as the royal road to the unconscious. The result has been
that in recent years there have been relatively few clinical or theoretical
studies of dreams and their place in analytic practice.

A most welcome exception to this trend has been the invaluable
contributions of Dr. Eugene Mahon.

Writing with the elegance and grace for which he is well known in
his role as one of the Country's most gifted poets, over the past several

years Dr. Mahon has published a series of remarkable papers that have enhanced our knowledge and understanding of dreams in a highly creative and clinically valuable way.

Whether providing a novel and insightful reading of Freud's classic study of dreams, writing about dreams within dreams, offering a remarkable account of one man's dreams from childhood to his sixth decade of life, or any of the other topics included in this essential volume. Eugene Mahon has offered us fresh and much needed insights into aspects of dream life that we regularly encounter in our clinical work.

The subjects that Dr. Mahon addresses have not been previously discussed in the illuminating way that characterizes his writing; and by bringing these seminal essays together in this volume, he has rendered a great service to the analytic community.

It is rare in our field for an author to explore a topic that not only is of interest to, and important for, analysts of every theoretical persuasion, but to do so in a way that adds to our knowledge of both the theory and the clinical application of the subject under discussion.

In this unique and important volume, Eugene Mahon has accomplished that rare feat. Reading it, I found, as I believe you will also, that I learned more about dreams in general and particular aspects of dreams that I knew little about, than I had since reading Freud's original work. To have such an experience is not only rare, but quite wonderful.

Eugene Mahon has given all of us a precious gift, one for which we are immensely grateful.

CONTENTS

Acknowledgements vii

Foreword ix

1. Freud and Dreaming.. 1

2. The Evolution of Dreams 29

3. Dreams within Dreams 69

4. Clarence's Dream in *Richard III*: A Dream within a Dream? 81

5. The Uncanny in a Dream 95

6. A Film in a Dream 105

7. A Parapraxis in a Dream 117

8. A Trick in a Dream... 125

9. A Joke in a Dream.. 139

10. A Pun in a Dream 143

11. A Cartoon in a Dream... 149

12. A Poem and A Dream.. 163

13. Trump Dreams.. 183

14. James Joyce and The Dream: A Psychoanalytic Inquiry 191

Epilogue 215

1

FREUD AND DREAMING

The title of this book, *Such Stuff as Dreams*, pays homage to Shakespeare's line from *The Tempest* "We are such stuff as dreams are made on and our little life is rounded with a sleep." Prospero's lines suggest that the stuff of dreams is as complexly magical as the stuff evolution has used to fashion the human "little life" out of a little life that "is rounded with a sleep." This is not a book about the evolution of dreams as a tactical strategy that centuries of evolutionary experiment have accomplished, a fascinating topic in and of itself that is beyond my ability to fathom or write coherently about. The closest I come to an evolutionary statement is in chapter two, on the dreams of one man from early childhood to his fiftieth year of life, but that is more of a developmental study than an evolutionary one.

Many aspects of the dream's singularity are raised for scrutiny. Does the dream have an exceptional status in psychoanalysis, making it the "royal road" to the unconscious, or is it merely one of many points of entry into the unconscious and its repressed mysteries? There are analysts who believe that the dream does indeed have an exceptional status in psychoanalysis since Freud's groundbreaking research on the dream secured a permanent place for it in the history of ideas. New scientific ground had been broken, an achievement that has weathered well for the last 120 years and has been confirmed over and over by scientists who have corroborated the usefulness of the discovery in their own work with one unique mind after another as they analyzed their patients.

"Insight such as this falls to one's lot but once in a lifetime." When Freud wrote this, in 1931, in the preface to the third (revised) English edition of *The Interpretation of Dreams*, he was fully aware of the contribution he had made to the history of ideas. The insights at the core of his magnum opus were hatched in the free-associative climate of a self-analysis he had labored on since 1895. "Labor" is the right term: the product that was born of that labor has weathered praise and criticism well for more than a century and still stands as a monument to what one scientist can achieve by studying a baffling product intensely. While Freud liked to see his extraordinary scholarship and the uniqueness of his discovery as part of an intellectual lineage, traceable back to Artemidorus and the Ancients, Peter Thonemann, in his important book on *Artemidorus' The Interpretation of Dreams* (2020), argues, that there are profound differences between Artemidorus's approach and Freud's. Artemidorus's book is important in its own right: he collected dreams all over Greece, Asia Minor, and Italy around AD 200. If the latent content of these dreams was not his concern, the manifest content alone is an extraordinary record of the sexual and aggressive wishes and concerns of a wide swath of the teeming society of the time. While it is an extraordinary record of the sexuality of the time, Thonemann points out that Freud is in search of the elusive latent content and the extraordinary distortions it must pass through before becoming a manifest mask of itself, whereas Artemidorus is content to record the manifest records only

Freud's achievement stands alone. While Sophocles, using Jocasta as his mouthpiece, suggests that many a man has slept with his mother in his dreams, he does not however supply the multiple meanings such manifest content may imply. Freud's raw material was himself: over a protracted period (1895 to 1899) he subjected his dreams to the deepest scrutiny.

2

What he achieved with his newly created free-associative method is well known, but let us review it briefly in this opening chapter.

Freud sensed that the manifest content was the result of a latent content that was disguised and distorted out of all recognition. He intuited that there must be what he called the *dream-work* orchestrating this metamorphosis of the latent dream thoughts into the distorted masquerade of the manifest content of a dream. A code was needed to facilitate the dream researcher as s/he tried to interpret. The discovery of that code was essentially found in the primary processes Freud intuited, which must be at the core of the distorting mirror that the dream-work employed to create a visual tableau that was practically unintelligible. Describing the primary processes of intelligence that inform the surrealism of unconscious mentation, Freud contrasted them with the more understandable secondary processes that shaped the realistic assessments of everyday life. By describing the primary processes of condensation, displacement, symbolism, and the need for the visual tableaux and dramatizations that replace words with images in the manifest content of dreams, he essentially exposed the cleverness of the dream-work's artistry and made it possible for dream interpreters to trace the distortions of manifest content back to the coherence of a latent content that has been so disguised. Why was such disguise so necessary? Freud believed that there was a dream censor that would never allow the wild sexual and aggressive content of latent dream thoughts to parade its lewd, murderous, incestuous wishes in the consciousness of dream content without blowing the whistle and scuttling the whole dream mise-en-scène lest nightmare ensues.

A dream sample will illustrate this process. I will use a dream that Freud used in *On Dreams* (1901), his shorter synopsis of the great magnum opus of 1900.

3

Company at table or table d'hôte... spinach was being eaten... Frau E.L. was sitting beside me; she was turning her whole attention to me and laid her hand on my knee in an intimate manner. I removed her hand unresponsively. She then said: "But you always had such beautiful eyes."...I then had an indistinct picture of two eyes, as though it were a drawing or like the outline of a pair of spectacles...

Freud then applies his interpretive method whereby he freely associates to every item in the dream. At first Freud is puzzled. Frau E.L. is a person he hardly knows. "Reflecting over this dream brought me no nearer to understanding it. I determined however to set down without any premeditation or criticism the associations which presented themselves to my observation." This act of freely associating to every detail of the dream content has remained the essential methodology for helping the patient, or the self, to go beyond manifest content and immerse themself in the latent content that spawned the dream.

Table d'hôte reminds Freud of a ride with a friend in a taxicab. Freud made a joke about the taximeter: you owe sixty hellers (about sixpence) even before the journey begins! This reminds him of a table d'hôte. "It makes me avaricious and selfish because it keeps reminding me of what I owe." This leads to Freud quoting from Goethe's Wilhelm Meister; addressing the heavenly powers, the quotation says: "You lead us into life, you make the poor creature guilty" or "you make the poor man fall into debt."

Then Freud goes on to a second association about table d'hôte. Freud was at a hotel in the Tyrol. His wife was not being "sufficiently reserved" toward some people Freud had no desire to be friendly with. By way of contrast Frau E.L had "turned her whole attention to" Freud. Further associations led to an episode between Freud and his wife when he was courting her and she gave him a caress under the table in response to a love letter he had sent her. But in the dream his wife was replaced by the "comparative stranger" Frau E.L.

Frau E.L. was the daughter of a man to whom Freud had once been in debt. Freud then associates to her having said to him in the dream: "You've always had such beautiful eyes," which Freud believes can only have meant: "People have always done everything for you for love." Then Freud connects this line of thought with the taxicab ride and his friend taking him home "without my paying for it." "It must have made an impression on me," Freud says. He continues to associate: whereas the friend whose guests we were yesterday has often put me in his debt, Freud had allowed an opportunity to repay him to slip by. "He has only had one present from me—an antique bowl, round which there are *eyes* painted: what is known as an "ochiale' to avert the evil eye." Moreover, this friend is an eye surgeon. That same evening Freud had sent a woman patient to him to fit her with spectacles.

Freud then associates to spinach: one of Freud's children, the one who really deserves to be admired for his "beautiful eyes" refused to eat any spinach! Freud then remembers how it was he as a child who had refused to eat spinach, showing how his own genetic life had made an entrance in the dream. Whereas the manifest content of the dream was "unemotional, disconnected, and unintelligible," the thoughts behind the dream were connected to "intense and well-founded affective impulses." The thoughts themselves fell into logical chains in which certain central ideas made their appearance more than once. "The contrast between 'selfish' and 'unselfish' and the elements 'being in debt' and 'without paying for it' were central ideas of this kind, not represented in the dream itself." Freud refuses to go further since "I should be obliged to betray many things which had better remain my secret." He states that he would have to reveal "a central nodal point" but that considerations of a personal and not of a scientific nature prevent his doing so in public.

It is hard not to be curious about the nodal point that Freud is refusing to disclose, but for his purposes, and indeed ours, he has illustrated beautifully what he wished to convey: how manifest content and latent content relate profoundly and emotionally to each other. Freud then poses two critical questions for himself: (1) What is the psychical process that has transformed the latent content of dream into the manifest one which is known to me from my memory? (2) What are the motive or motives that have necessitated this transformation? He proposes to call the process that transforms the latent into the manifest content the "dream-work" and the process that tries to transform the disguised manifest content back into the latent content that spawned it the work of analysis.

He then discusses how the dream-work uses primary processes to distort logical sequential rational secondary process thinking into the disguised exasperating unintelligible disorder of a manifest dream. He describes how condensation, displacement, and the need for dramatization and representability derail the typical verbal logic of secondary process reasoning into the distorted surreal phantasmagoria of typical dreams and memory's struggle to retain them and subject them to inquiry.

Freud notes that if one assembles all the dream thoughts that the free-associative work on the manifest content has produced, the sheer volume of such verbal excavation would dwarf the relatively few images that comprise the totality of the manifest representation of the dream. Comparing the two, he argues that the latent dream thoughts have been compressed dramatically to force-fit into the minimalism of manifest dream story. This compression or condensation is the basic labor of the dream-work: by compressing so much it makes the composite imagery of the dream *overdetermined*. A single dream image may be a composite of so many dream thoughts *condensed* into one. Freud uses Galton's work on composite photography as an analogy. Sir Francis Galton showed how one single photograph could be in actuality many images compressed or condensed into one. Using the table d'hôte specimen dream, Freud shows how such compression works. One of the ideas stirred up by the dream was the wish "I should like to get some enjoyment without cost." "Kosten" is the German word for "cost," but kosten in German can mean either "cost" or "to taste." This connects to the spinach being served in the dream. But when children refuse to eat their spinach, the mother will urge the child to at least just "taste it." "It may seem strange that the dream-work should make such free use of verbal ambiguity," Freud writes, but his point is that such compression of imagery and verbal ambiguity is really one of the hallmarks of the dreaming process.

Freud suggests that if condensation is one of the main tools at the disposal of the dream-work as it transforms latent intelligible ideas into what appears to be nonsense, the dream-work has an even more potent agent of disguise in what Freud calls dream-displacement. Freud compares this particular psychic strategy to Nietzsche's phrase "a transvaluation of psychical values." The phrase comes from Nietzsche's book *The Antichrist*, in which he criticizes Christianity for its devaluation of human instinctual exuberance and desire, claiming that instinct is sin! In other words, the beauty of life-affirming human instinct is deplored and replaced by the dehumanizing concept of sin. Freud explains this displacement of psychical values in the following way: "In the course of the dream-work, the psychical intensity passes over from the thoughts and ideas to which it properly belongs on to others which in our judgment have no claim to any such emphasis." Using the table d'hôte dream again as an illustration of displacement at work, he shows how the insignificant event of his friend giving him a free ride in a cab gets attached to issues of great significance. Freud had actually compared the taximeter cab with the table d'hôte menu, whereby in both cases you owe money even before you get started! Freud then shows that these trivialities, derived from the day's residue, have a deeper connection to a far more serious consideration. A few days earlier, Freud had paid out a considerable sum of money on behalf of a family member whom he was very fond of. Freud writes: "No wonder, said the dream thoughts, if this person were to feel grateful to me: love of that sort would not be 'free of cost.'" Nietzsche's transvaluation of psychical values and Freud's concept of dream-displacement have elevated the trivial to a significance it does not deserve, while at the same time diminishing the status of the truly significant. And, of course, condensation and displacement can work in tandem, making the dream-work's mischief even more obfuscating so that the resultant manifest content is more baffling than ever.

Another aspect of dream distortion that Freud accentuated was the dream-work's insistence on replacing verbal exposition with pictorial representations so much so that elaborate verbal unconscious dream thoughts can be captured in a single image or two. In chapter seven of *The Interpretation of Dreams*, Freud's picket fence analogy depicted the verbal world of secondary process being changed utterly into the pictorial by the regressive forces that characterize the dream state. Silberer had documented something very similar when he noticed that as the drowsy mind begins to slip into sleep, a process of transforming words into images has begun already even before the dreaming process has established itself fully in the REM compartments of sleep. Falling asleep this is a relatively common regressive event that anyone on the verge of sleep can confirm for her or his self.

Freud also described a process of secondary revision in which loose ends are tied up as the whole jumble of manifest images is pulled together so that a coherent—or almost coherent—dream story line can be articulated by an awakened dreamer. Sometimes this is impossible, and even telling the ungraspable elements of the dream to another seems impossible.

Dreams use symbolism also as an overdetermined shorthand that assists the compression that condensation accomplishes. The symbolic in dreams has been controversial. Some see symbols as fixed entities that convey only one meaning: stairs represent rising sexual tension! Others see symbols as overdetermined entities that can represent whatever the unconscious needs them to represent, a complexity that only the free-associative work of each analysand can determine.

Freud's intuitions and insights, and his extraordinary codebreaking discovery of the primary processes of condensation, displacement, symbolism, and the skill of transforming the verbal into imagistic representations of itself made it possible for dream interpreters to make sense out of the most complexly distorted dream experience. Freud's discovery of free associations as affording even greater access to unconscious mentation than hypnosis did had the added advantage that the analysand became the critical ally of the analyst as the dream was being dissected and the manifest disguise was being translated into the latent revelation hidden so expertly behind it. The free associations of the patient became the sine qua non of dream interpretation: the analyst may be the guide but the dreamer/patient led the way into the chaos of dream as more and more associations suggested links between the past and the present, between the days' residues and forgotten genetic events, basically between childhood and the current status of development and experience.

Now that Freud had discovered how the code of enigmatic disguise worked, he could apply what he had unearthed for further excavations of his own dreams. The self-analysis of his dreams led to remarkable discoveries that I would like to turn to now. I want to suggest that between the death of his father and his discovery of the Oedipus complex in October 1897, he threw open the doors of the unconscious in a revolutionary manner. I have argued that it was the combination of mourning and dreaming in that crucial year that made the unconscious mind so creatively available to him. Mourning can be described as an inexorable process whereby the reality of one's loss is pitted against resurrections of the loss in hallucinatory moments of grief as reality and denial of unacceptable reality are pitted against one another in the conflicted theater of the mind. In Freud's case, the work of mourning was a process whereby the image of the dead father had to be divested of all the libidinal energy housed in it, and that emotional energy had to be then invested in the living, loving entities around him. One of those most significant relationships would have been with his mother. If Freud was basically being asked to diminish or abolish his relationship with his father and reinvest it in his mother, he was basically involved in an oedipal struggle before he discovered what an oedipal struggle was! My contention is that it was actually these internal processes of mourning and dreaming in the year between his father's death and the discovery of the Oedipus complex in 1897 that allowed Freud to painfully arrive at his momentous discovery. Dreaming is an attempt to establish the hegemony of the infantile wish while mourning attempts to arrive at the acceptance of the reality of loss and death. They are diametrically opposed in their unconscious missions. I believe that out of that fundamental clash came the discovery of the Oedipus complex.

It is time to examine those dreams that Freud had in the year after his father's death, eleven dreams that provided him with all the clues he needed to unearth his momentous discovery.

Before his announcement of his discovery to Fliess in 1897, there are a dozen well-documented dreams that could be thought of as stepping-stones on the road to discovery:

1. The Irma's Injection Dream (July 24, 1895).
2. The Close the Eyes Dream (October 25–26, 1896).
3. The Four Rome Dreams (January 1897).
4. The Uncle with the Yellow Beard Dream (February 1897).
5. The Villa Secerno Dream (April 27–28, 1897).
6. The Hella Dream (May 1897).
7. The Running Upstairs Undressed Dream (May 1897).

8.   The Sheep's Head Dream (October 3–4, 1897).

9.   One-Eyed Doctor Dream (October 1897).

If we omit the Irma's injection dream (July 24, 1895), the other eleven dreams were dreamed in the year between the death of Freud's father and the discovery of the Oedipus complex. These dreams have been analyzed well by Freud himself and later by Grinstein and Anzieu. These eleven dreams were some of the essential raw materials of Freud's intense self-analysis during that most fruitful year, nocturnal gifts he extracted from sleep and his capacity to remember his dreams. But while he was awake there was an essential context to be considered as well. If we try to track Freud's unconscious affects from the Irma Dream to the One Eyed Doctor Dream, I believe we will be like the ancient audience at Sophocles's Oedipus Rex awash in dramatic irony as they witness the doomed hero (Oedipus) doggedly and innocently insisting on pursuing a truth that only the audience knows will destroy him! Freud, of course, was not destroyed by his discovery, like Oedipus, but enlightened.

I will try to summarize the dreams and their main affects as I try to depict the structure of the Oedipus complex as it slowly emerges from the mists of ignorance. I will treat the sequence of dreams as if their partial insights eventually coalesce to make the ultimate creative eureka of insight possible. I will assume that the reader has a certain familiarity with these dreams, and that memory can be refreshed, if necessary, by access to the original text and subsequent commentary (Freud, Anzieu, Grinstein, to name a few).

The Irma Dream is probably the most famous of Freud's dreams, brilliantly deconstructed by Freud himself and the subject of much further exegesis by a host of subsequent investigators. I will make one comment only: the predominant affect is guilt about the botched surgery, Freud's reluctance to blame Fliess directly for his obvious surgical mismanagement of the case and Freud's wish to exonerate himself from guilt by association. The elements of an oedipal triangle are all there: a damaged woman (Irma), a guilty man (Fliess), a child witness (Freud); but Freud has no inkling of their oedipal meaning yet. His mind seems focused on the challenge and complexity of the dreaming process and how to make sense out of it.

The Close the Eyes Dream is obviously about Jacob Freud's death, since we know it was dreamed either immediately before the death or very soon thereafter. The manifest content is stark: "You are requested to close the eyes (or close an eye)." This sentence, like an announcement on a signpost, is the only content of the dream. The conflict seems obvious: Should Freud recognize his guilt about his father's death, face it squarely, or close an eye to it, wink at it?

The Four Rome Dreams: if we compress these most complex dreams together, they express the wish to get to Rome, a very overdetermined desire of Freud's, to get to Rome like Hannibal (a one-eyed hero) and thereby overcome the shame he felt when his father was humiliated on the street by a Christian. Freud has described that childhood humiliation:

> I may have been ten or twelve years old, when my father began to take me with him on his walks and reveal to me in his talk his views upon things in the world we live in. Thus it was, on one such occasion, that he told me a story to show me how much better things were now than they had been in his days. "When I was a young man," he said, "I went out for a walk one Saturday in the streets of your birthplace; I was well dressed and had a new fur cap on my head. A Christian came up to me and with a single blow knocked off my cap into the mud and shouted: 'Jew! Get off the pavement.'"
>
> "And what did you do?" I asked. "I went into the roadway and picked up my cap," was his quiet reply. This struck me as unheroic

12

conduct on the part of the big, strong man who was holding the little boy by the hand. I contrasted this situation with another that fitted my feelings better: the scene in which Hannibal's father, Hasdrubal, made his boy swear before the household altar to take vengeance on the Romans. Ever since that time Hannibal had had a place in my phantasies' (p. 197).

Freud later recognized his error: he has confused Hannibal's father Hamilcar Barca with Hannibal's brother Hasdrubal. This parapraxis is comparable to the one Freud made when he describes his discovery of the Oedipus complex for the first time in his letter to Fliess of October 15, 1897. Freud is comparing Hamlet and Oedipus Rex. Freud writes that Hamlet is "positively precipitate in murdering Laertes." A close reading of Shakespeare makes it clear that the "positive precipitate" murder refers to Polonius, not Laertes. A father and a son are being confused in this slip. Could it be that the discoverer of the Oedipus complex flinches as he imagines the oedipal death of his own father and that his guilt-inspired slip unconsciously dispatches himself (Jacob's son) instead, Polonius's son Laertes an unconscious stand-in for Freud himself? (Ironically, it was Laertes who killed Hamlet in act 5, having connived with Claudius to get revenge on the man who had killed Laertes's father, Polonius). The fact that all of this was first adumbrated in a letter to the transferential Fliess adds to the oedipal irony in question.

The Uncle with the Yellow Beard Dream: Freud's ambition to become a professor is the core affect of this dream.

The Villa Secerno Dream. Obvious growing ambivalence toward Fliess and toward his own father begins to emerge more clearly in this dream. Secerno refers to hiding or secreting, the conflict about knowing and not knowing; opening the eyes or closing them continues to be unresolved.

The Hella Dream. Freud's sexual feeling for his daughter Mathilde is the main affect of the dream. Jones maintains that this dream led to Freud's abandonment of the seduction hypothesis. This is a major advance: sexual instincts must be acknowledged as opposed to projected or disavowed.

The Running Up the Stairs Undressed Dream. This is the dream along with other staircase dreams that leads to the recovery of a most significant memory of Monica Zajic, the nurse who took care of Freud in Freiberg. This nurse could be rough. As Freud sarcastically puts it: "her treatment of me was not always excessive in amiability." So if the Villa Secerno Dream allows Freud to embrace his ambivalence toward Fliess and his father, this retrieved memory puts him in touch with ambivalence toward a woman. The two poles of the Oedipus complex (positive and negative oedipal attitudes toward parents) are beginning to come into view.

The Sheep's Head Dream. Here is the manifest content:

1. I took out a subscription in S. and R.'s bookshop for a periodical costing twenty florins a year.
2. She was my teacher in sexual matters and complained because I was clumsy and unable to do anything...At the same time I saw the skull of a small animal and in the dream I thought "pig," but in the analysis I associated it with your wish (Fliess's) that I might find as Goethe once did, a skull on the Lido to enlighten me. But I did not find it. So I was a 'little block head' (Ein kleiner schafskopf, a little sheep's-head).

This dream leads to the memory of the nurse who bathed him in red water (she was menstruating). She also stole twenty zehners, a "crime" Freud first took on himself. Later his mother confirmed the details of his retrieved memory but corrected his distortion. The nurse was found out and subsequently spent ten months in prison. Freud was clearly affected by the loss of this significant primary object. Trying to assess the significance of a recently recovered memory, Freud writes: "I said to myself that if the old woman disappeared from my life so suddenly, it must be possible to demonstrate the impression this made on me. Where is it, then? Thereupon a scene occurred to me which in the course of twenty-five years has occasionally emerged in my conscious memory without my understanding it." Freud is knocking on the door of the Oedipus complex, so to speak, and the door is about to be thrown open. Freud continues, remembering the frantic affects of the scene that returns to consciousness again and again without being fully understood. "My mother was nowhere to be found: I was crying in despair. My brother Philipp (twenty years older than I) unlocked a wardrobe (Kasten) for me, and when I did not find my mother inside it either, I cried even more until, slender and beautiful, she came in through the door." There is a poignant congruence here between a child trying to open the mystery of his own distorted magical misunderstandings and a genius trying to make science out of that distortion many years later. Freud did eventually make sense out of this memory and its condensation of the nurse being locked up in prison and his mother locked up in the prison of his own imaginings. Freud had feared that his mother was pregnant and was relieved when she appeared "slender and beautiful" and therefore decidedly not pregnant.

The components of the Oedipus complex were slowly falling into place: Philipp, the twenty-years-older brother, Freud's mother, and Freud himself locked in an oedipal unconscious "box" that only insight—and a most transgressive insight at that—could unlock. When one considers Freud's letter to Fliess of October 3, 1897 (which contains the Sheep's Head Dream in a postscript), it is clear that Freud's self-analysis had helped him to recover very early memories from the first three years of life. In that letter he admits to feeling jealous of his father, even if he had failed to find any evidence in the coffers of retrieved memory of sexual seduction

15

on the part of his father. He acknowledges sexual feelings for his *matrem*, whom he had seen "nudam" on a journey to Vienna with her when he was between "two and two and a half years." The need to describe his memory in Latin surely suggests his discomfort with the affects his oedipal conflict was arousing in him. In that same letter, Freud describes the birth of his brother Julius and the ill wishes he felt toward him. When Julius died a few months later, Freud's guilt must have been intense. Recounting all of this to Fliess in October 1897, on the verge of discovering the Oedipus complex, one senses that Julius was the prototype of oedipal hatred toward the father, given the telescopic, tendentious nature of memory.

The One-Eyed Doctor and Schoolmaster Dream. Here is the manifest content:

I had a dream of someone who I knew in my dream was the doctor in my native town. His face was indistinct but was confused with one of my masters at the secondary school, whom I still meet occasionally.

Freud had much resentment toward the childhood doctor. Freud's ambivalence is displayed by juxtaposing the hated doctor and the beloved schoolmaster. These condensations became clearer when his mother explained to Freud that both doctor and schoolmaster were one-eyed! Freud seems very reluctant to interpret this dream fully when he first describes it to Fliess. It is only in later editions of *The Interpretation of Dreams* that Freud allows himself to disclose how he had fallen as a very young child and injured his chin. The castration fear aspect of the Oedipus complex was too much to be incorporated into the complexity of Freud's emerging philosophy at this time. His mother reminded him of the reason the one-eyed doctor had been called in the first place. It is tempting to condense the one-eyed doctor and the closing of one eye in the earlier

"It is necessary to close the eyes/an eye, dream." Freud's oedipal hatred of the one-eyed doctor and father can only be insightfully seen with both eyes open. Closing one eye or two at this point would be a denial of an extraordinary insight at the moment of incipient triumph. Freud's question in *Mourning and Melancholia* is relevant in this context. "Why, then, after it has run its course, is there no hint in its case (Freud is referring to mourning, and when the work of mourning is completed) of the economic condition for a phase of triumph?" Freud immediately writes: "I find it impossible to answer this objection straight away." If I am correct in my thesis that mourning contains in its very form and structure the architecture of the Oedipus complex itself (the very discovery Freud was on the verge of granting himself in October 1897), he must have felt it almost impossible to experience any sense of triumph, especially if that triumph were in any way related to an oedipal "good riddance" triumph. "Aha"s of excitement and "Eureka"s of self-congratulation usually accompany great discovery. In Freud's case was it necessary to close the eyes to such oedipal dancing on his father's grave? Freud insisted on depicting the Close the Eyes Dream as a twofold text: to close one eye (to wink) is juxtaposed with the closing of both eyes. To wink at someone has an oedipal meaning that I would like to emphasize. Freud did not focus on this; nor did subsequent scholarship, to the best of my knowledge. If one deconstructs the drama of one person winking at another in the presence of a third, it becomes clear that an oedipal motif is being enacted. Winking is usually triadic. I wink at you, both of us in a collusion of supposed superiority over a third party who is left out of our mutual comic conspiracy against him. Isn't winking a drama of ironic subtlety, a cruel version of the Oedipus complex in comic dress, two "informed" members lording it over an unwitting third?

There is one other "incident" prior to Freud's discovery of the Oedipus complex that is analogous to winking and closing the eyes or keeping them insightfully open. Between October 4 and 15, Freud made a professional blunder. He used to see an old woman daily to put a few drops of eye lotion (collyrium) into her eye and give her a morphine injection. (Is it not striking how prominent eyes are in Freud's mind as he approaches this most momentous discovery, as if he needs to blind himself like Oedipus even as he dares to retrace the footsteps of Sophocles's tragic protagonist?) This particular morning he put morphine in the eye instead of collyrium. It was only years later in *The Psychopathology of Everyday Life* that Freud explained his symptomatic act. It was a memory of a patient's dream that made it possible for Freud to understand the meaning of his self-destructive, mal-practical parapraxis.

"I was under the influence of a dream which had been told me by a young man the previous evening and the content of which could only point to sexual intercourse with his mother. (…) While absorbed in thoughts of this kind, I came to my patient, who is over ninety, and I must have been on the way to grasping the universal human application of the Oedipus myth as correlated with the Fate which is revealed in the oracles; for at that point I did violence to or committed a blunder on 'the old woman.'"

Freud was aware in October 1897 that he was "on the way to grasping the human application of the Oedipus myth," but he seemed to need to blind not only the old woman whom he transgressed against but himself as well, by damaging his professional status in a kind of oedipal blinding of himself. His tragic identification with Oedipus seems total at such moments of blinding insight, even as his scientific integrity insists on staying the course.

It is time to reflect on how the dream has fared in psychoanalytic theory and clinical practice since 1900. There is no question that dreams have become a cornerstone of clinical practice. Freud's *Interpretation of Dreams* and its many revisions since its first appearance in 1900 has been firmly established as the essential text for clinicians to apply in their own unique ways of course. Whether dreams have an exceptional status or are no more important, nor less important, than all the other psychological items free associations people the analytic process within the course of an analysis has been disputed.

Ralph Greenson in 1970 claimed that "the dream is an exceptional and unique production of the patient. It is his special creation but can only be fully understood if the analyst and the patient work together by means of the patient's free associations and the analyst's interpretations. To work effectively with a patient's dream the analyst must subordinate his own theoretical interests, his own personal curiosity, and attempt to make contact with what is living, accessible, and dominant in the patient's psychic life at the time. He must associate empathically, with the patient's material, as if he had lived the patient's life. Then he must translate the pictures he gets from the patient's verbal rendering of the dream back into thoughts, ideas, and words. Finally, he must ask himself what of all of this will be valuable to the patient's conscious and reasonable ego and how he can say it effectively to the patient."

This is very similar to Freud's method of analyzing the table d'hôte dream described earlier. Greenson describes recent work with a patient of his own in a very moving and convincing manner. He calls the patient Mr. M. He's a thirty-year-old writer who came seeking treatment for a constant sense of underlying depressiveness, frequent anxiety in social and sexual situations, and a feeling of being a failure despite considerable success in his profession and what appeared to be a good relationship with his wife and children. His first dream in the sixth week is reported as follows:

I was making a phone call to some guy in a men's clothing store. I had ordered some clothes made to order and they didn't fit. I asked the guy to take them back, but he said I had to come in myself. I told him I was not going to pay for the clothes until they fit. I said it seems like you just took them off the rack. I repeated, I won't pay for the clothes until they fit. As I said that, I began to vomit, so I dropped the phone and ran into the bathroom to wash out my mouth. I left the receiver dangling, and I could hear the guy saying "What did you say? What? What?"

The patient freely associates to the vomiting. He never vomits. The last time must have been in childhood, but he has no memory of it. He then blurts out: "Free association is like vomiting!" The analyst interprets: "Yes, free association becomes like vomiting when things are trying to come up in your mind that you would rather keep inside yourself and away from me. The dream says it has to do with something not fitting you properly." The patient quickly replied, "Yes, it's about clothes, but that is too silly. Why clothes? Clothes not fitting?" (Pause) "Oh my God, this can't have anything to do with the analysis. The man saying, 'What is it? What? What?' that could be you." (Pause) "I leave you talking and go to vomit in the bathroom—but why, why do I do that?" The analyst answers, "When I give you an interpretation that doesn't fit you, you must resent it and feel that I just took it off my 'psychoanalytic rack,' like the 'textbooky' analysts you have heard about." The patient agrees, saying, "You are right. When you say things that don't seem to fit me, sometimes I do get annoyed, but I keep it in." (Pause) "I get scared here when I feel angry. It's like being afraid of my father when I was a kid." (Pause) "I now suddenly see a vague picture of me vomiting when I was about three or four years old." (Pause) "It was my mother, right on her. She must have been holding me. She was so nice about it, too, she took me to the bathroom and cleaned me up and herself too. Amazing this whole thing." The analyst comments: "Yes, apparently you were not afraid to vomit things up in front of your mother, but you must have been very afraid of doing that with your father, and now you feel the same way here with me. But you see, these kinds of things do tend to come up or in such things like your forgetting to pay me this month."

The patient was startled by this uncanny unconscious collusion between parapraxis, dream, and transference. He was startled and blurted out: "This is too much. I had your check in my wallet, but at the last minute I decided to change my jacket and left my wallet at home. And I never thought of it when I was telling you the dream, all about not wanting to pay that man. Something must really be cooking in me."

This is a beautiful example of a patient's free associations coupled with an analyst's intuitive collaboration working with a dream and extracting exciting insights from it.

Greenson describes a second dream that occurred two and a half years later. The patient had to interrupt his analysis because of an assignment abroad but had returned home some three months before the dream. He was in a chronic state of quiet, passive depression. The analyst had interpreted this as a reaction to his wife's fourth pregnancy, which must have stirred up memories and feelings in regard to his mother's three pregnancies after his birth. It seemed clear to the analyst that he was reexperiencing the loss of the feeling and fantasies of being his mother's favorite, the only child and the favorite child. Mr. M. accepted Greenson's interpretations submissively, conceding that they had merit, even though he could recall nothing about the birth of his three siblings, nor of his reactions, although he was over six when the youngest was born. The analyst concedes that the interpretation had had little effect on the patient's mood. But a little later in the process, Mr. M sadly and quietly and in a somewhat mournful tone told the following dream.

I am in a huge store, a department store. There are lots of shiny orange and green plastic raincoats on display. A middle-aged Jewish woman is arranging other articles of clothing. Nearby is a female manikin dressed in a gray flannel dress. I go outside and see a woman who looks very familiar but I can't say specifically who she is. She is waiting expectantly and eagerly for me near a small surrey, putting clothes in it. I feel sorry for the poor horse and then realize the surrey is detached from the horse. I lift up the surrey to connect it and I am surprised how light the surrey is, but I don't know how to hitch it up to the horse. I also realize then that it was silly to feel sorry for the horse.

The patient associates to the elements in the dream: he has had no sex with his wife and feels lonely in his own big house, which he worked like a horse to pay for. "Maybe I am the horse in the dream I feel sorry for," he says mournfully. The analyst makes a most creative intervention at this point. The analyst senses that the surrey is a disguised baby buggy, repressed for many years in the patient's amnesia. The analyst does not want to push the point, so he slyly calls the surrey a buggy to see what the patient might make of it. The analyst says: "You think you are the horse that had such a big load to carry, but then you lift up the buggy and you are surprised to discover how light it is." The patient interrupts: "That buggy is so light, it's a baby buggy. It's a baby carriage. No wonder it was so light, and so tiny, and the woman was putting clothes on it, like diapers." The analyst interrupts and says: "A baby buggy is very heavy for a little boy, he has to work like a horse to push it." Mr. M burst in with, "I can remember trying to push my baby sister in her buggy but it was too heavy for me. Now I see my father carrying the baby carriage downstairs as if it were a toy. I can even remember my brother and me together trying to push it." The analyst interprets and reconstructs: "I believe you have been depressed ever since your wife got pregnant because it stirred up memories of how you reacted when you were a small boy and your mother got pregnant and delivered your brother and sisters. You didn't want to face the fact that your father was hitched up to the coming of the babies. You wished you could have been the father of the babies. But you weren't—you didn't know how to do it as a little boy and you felt left out in the cold, detached. You have been depressed about this ever since." Mr. M responded: "I've always felt like I'm not a real man. I act like one, but inside I still feel a real man should be like my father; strong physically, tough, and unafraid. I can fly airplanes but my hands sweat whenever I want to screw my own wife."

In the next hour of the analysis, the meaning of the green and orange became clear. Mr. M remembers jokes from his adolescence in which the terms "raincoats" and "rubbers" were used to refer to condoms. He then remembered finding condoms in his father's chest of drawers and later stealing some for his own use, just in case an opportunity presented itself, which, he wistfully said, didn't occur for several years. By that time the rubbers—the raincoats—had disintegrated in his wallet. The shiny new raincoats in the dream represented wish fulfillment!

Greenson reports lots of other interesting commentaries on these two dreams, including his sense that he too was the poor horse who had the patient as a big load to carry and also that the analyst was the "horse's ass" who could not help Mr. M make a proper sexual connection with his wife or any other woman. While there is much more to focus on in this rich analytic material, I believe I have extracted from Greenson's analytic process the basic point he is stressing: dreams are exceptional in the way they condense genetic material, transference, symptoms and the way an astute, creative, sensitive analyst whose unconscious mind is incredibly attuned to the free-associative process can "play" with the process to extraordinary effect. But I want to stress also that there are other exceptional roads that lead to the unconscious citadel and that there is no need to identify only one royal road to the unconscious.

There is another case in the psychoanalytic literature that bears out what Greenson is describing. Battin and Mahon (2003), in an article entitled "Symptom, Screen Memory, and Dream," describe an analysand whose screen memory in which her sister, while teaching her to swim, seemed to be drowning her was also reflected in a symptom in which she couldn't breathe on the couch, essentially an enactment of childhood experiences of choking sensations. All of these genetic events could be worked on after free associations brought them into the transference/countertransference process, in general, and into one dream in particular. In the dream the patient was drowning and people could not help because their arms were not long enough. As psychoanalytic process deepened, the screen memory, the dream, and the symptom seemed to *converse* with each other. The genetic past, the symptomatic past, the "drowning" dream, and a transference reaction in which the analyst was "drowning" the analysand with insights she did not always feel she was able to process were all associations to each other as the analysis deepened. In the first part of the "drowning" dream, the dreamer described a complicated series of wires that would administer an electric shock to others, which gave the dreamer a lot of pleasure. The patient told this segment of the dream first even though it was the drowning segment that she had actually dreamed first. It was clear that the patient, after years of analysis, was ready to acknowledge that it was her aggression, transformed earlier into reaction formations of piety and passivity, that connected the symptom, the screen memory, and the dream together. It was this kind of established connectivity and integration that allowed the analysand to finish her analysis with a renewed sense of vigor and exuberance as her ego reclaimed all the affects it had formerly felt were more safely housed in superego and id.

I have described this rich psychoanalytic process in an extremely truncated form: I wanted to corroborate the kind of communion between transference, forgotten genetic memory, current experience, and dream that Greenson has described so eruditely and passionately with another example of psychoanalytic process that showed how the past and present could become fluid enough in analytic process to allow significant working through of *far-fetched* material so that adaptive psychic change could be achieved.

It is time to end this chapter in which I have introduced the intuitions of Sigmund Freud that allowed the most baffling dreams to reveal their secrets. Freud's discovery of free associations, coupled with his ingenious sense that dream-work and its clever deployment of primary process thinking, made it possible to go beyond the sleight of hand of manifest trickery and expose the dream-work's artistry by undoing the distortions that primary processes (condensation, displacement, symbolism, word transformation into images, the need for representability and secondary revision) had wrought. I also showed how Freud used his own interpretive skills to analyze the eleven dreams that followed his father's death. I argued that two very different psychic processes, his mourning and his dreaming, led him eventually to articulate the dynamic elements of the Oedipus complex, a discovery that has remained at the core of psychoanalytic thinking ever since.

Freud's discoveries have withstood the test of time. Psychoanalysts have interpreted dreams for more than a hundred years using Freud's groundbreaking discoveries and incorporating them into their own unique style of clinical expertise. The basic theory and principles need no further elaboration. In the subsequent chapters of this book, I hope to elaborate on loose ends in Freud's magnum opus and challenge some ideas when it seems that challenge is called for. The next chapter traces the evolution of dreams over a fifty-year period in one dreamer's life. I describe dreams from age four, age thirteen, age nineteen, age thirty, and age fifty and try to follow the uncanny continuity that inform quite different moments in a man's development.

I then try to concentrate on those areas where something new can be said. For example, Freud described dreams within dreams briefly in the first edition of *The Interpretation of Dreams*. I expand quite a bit on his ideas and introduce a new way of understanding the two portions of a dream within a dream. In the subsequent chapter on Clarence's dream in *Richard III*, I pose the question of whether Clarence's elaborate dream is best thought of as a dream within a dream. In the chapter called A Film in a Dream (followed by two subsequent examples of films in dreams), I question why the dream-work needed to employ the illusion of film since all dreams are pretty cinematic enough already.

Where Freud had argued that jokes in dreams are never really well-rendered jokes that make you laugh, I describe a joke in a dream that is actually quite witty and funny. I try to explain why the dream-work went to the trouble of constructing such a joke. I continue in that fashion, describing novel dreams that seem worthy of investigation. A Pun in a Dream, for example, shows how the most ingenious pun is used for cunning obfuscation and deceptive intent. Similarly, I show how the uncanny in a dream can startle the dreamer as he tries to understand the deceptive flourish and its tendentious raison d'être. A Parapraxis in a Dream, I argue, tries to gather the attention of dreamer and interpreter so that much more serious dream content can be neglected or ignored. A Cartoon in a Dream is a chapter that attempts to show why such a pictorial representation would be co-opted by the dream-work in the service of disguise. In A Trick in a Dream, I apply the same kind of questioning to try to explain what function the dream trick is serving. The chapter The Uncanny in a Dream is truly *uncanny*. The dreamer dreams of the name of a fictitious novelist only to discover that the novelist is an actual published novelist whose name has a very particular dynamic function in the dream. The chapter A Poem and a Dream tries to show how a poem, written right after a dream has been remembered, has a defensive as well as an interpretive dynamic current running through it. Both seem like extraordinary esthetic products that have some uncanny, and not so easily deciphered, dynamic contiguity. Toward the end of the book, in a chapter called James Joyce Dream Interpreter, I describe Joyce's fascination with dreams, his own and his wife's and friends'. Joyce expressed an antipathy toward Freud in his commentaries, but nevertheless it is clear that he was influenced by the father of psychoanalysis! The chapter Trump Dreams shows how the political climate can be a fertile days' residue for the formation of the manifest content of a dream. A most provocative political figure can be insinuated into the fabric of a dream for dynamic and defensive reasons that have more to do with psychodynamic political conflicts than current events.

2

THE EVOLUTION OF DREAMS

Introduction

A record of dreams of the same patient from four years of age to fifty became possible when a child analysand reported a dream in analysis at age four (the analysis lasted from age four and a half to age nine) and then returned for brief visits at ages thirteen, twenty, and thirty and then at almost fifty years of age, when he returned for a more sustained analytic engagement. I will present the six dreams first, then give a description of the child analysis that lasted from age four and a half to age nine, then cite the ensuing dreams with as much clinical context as possible. (There is actually a seventh dream from early adolescence that Alex reported at age fifty, which will also be discussed.)

The Six Dreams

The First Dream (Age Four)

There is an octopus. As big as the Empire State Building. I had a stick. It (the octopus) swallowed me. I was fighting it. It spat me out.

The Second Dream (Age Thirteen)

I was running in the woods. Snakes appear. They come close to my face. I run and run. There are other children younger than I playing nearby. I try to make the snakes go in their direction.

The Third Dream (Age Twenty)

I am in a Batmobile. Batman is driving. I'm in the back seat. The Batmobile is not all it's cracked up to be. We are trying to chase some bad guys. We are slow to pull out of the garage in pursuit because we have to make several broken U-turns just to get out of the driveway. Finally we get going. I take the wheel. Eventually we catch up with the bad guys. We follow them over a desert and give chase 'round and 'round an oval.

The Fourth Dream (Age Thirty)

Infant falling out of plane. Plane escaping from aborigines. I look back in rearview mirror to catch a glimpse of infant if I can. I am copilot. Captain angry at me for looking back.

The Fifth Dream (Age Almost Fifty)

Wearing shirt with blue sticking tape attached to it. I try to pull it off. Cannot get it off me.

The Sixth Dream (Age Almost Fifty)

With Jared Kushner's brother. He is engaged in a real estate deal that Trump is involved with also. Our information can help Trump. So we meet Trump on football field. I am looking up to/at him.

Synopsis of the Child Analysis

The child's (let us call him Alexander) parents sought help for their four-and-a-half-year-old for a variety of symptoms, some of which they had noticed, some brought to their attention by the nursery school. The parents, sophisticated, analyzed people (mother was a successful artist; father ran his own lucrative advertising firm) who had firsthand knowledge of psychoanalysis and what it could offer as well as what it could not, sensed that their contributions to Alex's developmental struggles were significant, disclosures they could make nondefensively. The mother was aware that her conflicts about the dangers of intimacy were reflected in Alex's restlessness and difficulties with quiet time in the nursery, his obligatory "activities" being a measure of his fear of more passive aims; the father, considerably older than his wife, was aware that his lifelong unresolved oedipal struggles with his father were being reenacted in his behavior with his son. The parents were refreshingly honest about their parental skills and weaknesses, and this helped create a climate of mutual respect that had a facilitating effect on the subsequent years of analysis. Child analysis is not just a collaboration between child and analyst but a collaboration between analyst and parents as well, which is crucial as the emotional complexity of the analysis proceeds. The parents were alarmed by Alex's boastfulness, boisterousness, lying, provocativeness; the school was alarmed by his unruliness and hyperactivity: he seemed to wear his castration anxiety on his sleeve, grabbing at the penises of other children

31

as if to acquire more of what he feared to lose. At nap time, while others slept or at least rested, he needed to be on the go, activity his only resource, it seemed, against the pressure of anxiety.

While in the playroom for the initial consultations, his words, deeds, drawings, and play began to reveal the seething unconscious energies that lay behind all of his symptomatic acts. He could be provocative, scatological one minute, presenting his anus in mock submission to the "baboon" that was "interviewing" him; another minute he could be telling a story and illustrating it coherently and cooperatively. If there was a desire to shock and provoke, there was also a clear wish to communicate, which made the prospects of induction into analysis slightly less daunting. His initial stories and illustrations describe small animals that leave home and have lots of adventures with huge adversaries. They usually have two psychological escape routes—the oral or the phallic. They eat up the universe or they try to become as big as it. Poignantly, the ant hero will make his way to the top of the Empire State Building, a preposterous King Kong mask bravely covering the terror of the little endangered face.

Here is a story, edited slightly, which prefigures much of his analysis and gives a good sense of the four-and-a-half-year-old, his terrors and his defenses, his hopes and desperations.

Once upon a time there was a bunny. He always wanted to go away from his father and mother. He had to go to the hospital because he was a bad bunny, and a gorilla ate his tail off. A great bull came running by his house, and he, the little bunny, wanted to teach the bull how to hop on two feet and act like a rabbit. He ate orange carrots and turned orange. Then he discovered if he ate clear carrots, he would turn purple. Then the little bunny played hide-and-seek with a dinosaur. Then he jumped from the top of a tree after eating a whole bunch of leaves. He discovered he could fly instead of

32

hopping. The very next day he discovered he could never, ever, ever land from his flying. And then he discovered that there was a boat down in the sea and he flew over to the ship and they pulled him down, but he flew up again and then he stopped flying with his wings and then he dropped down into the ship. So the next day he discovered that the word "Alex" was spelled two hundred years ago "F-r-e-d," and the very, very, very next day in 1966, he discovered "Alex" was spelled "A-l-e-x." Then the very next day he wanted to eat all the bucktooth rabbits that were smaller than his mother and father and him. He wanted to eat every single thing in the whole country of New York, so that day he wanted to eat every word that wouldn't make sense, so he got so impressed at talking that he did not want to talk anymore. So he never, ever, ever came back home to his family.

The story is rich in dynamic meanings, so much so that the subsequent five years of analysis could be thought of as a series of associations to the profound themes raised in a seemingly lighthearted manner behind the masks of fiction. A full exploration of all the psychodynamic threads that informed this story and weaved their way into the psychoanalysis and beyond it into all the subsequent dreams is the ambitious goal of this article. The story is "convenient" from an anamnestic point of view since it paints such a vivid picture of a young mind's struggles with size, castration, impulses (flying), control (the ship), identity (Alex, Fred), identification (could the bunny learn to run like the bull? Could the bull learn to hop like the bunny?), etc. As an opening statement about the analytic situation and whether it is safe to bring words and play and dreams to it, the child's ambivalence seems palpable. One interpretation of the text could be constructed as follows: "If I leave home, I may never return. If I eat, there may be consequences. If I fly, I may not be able to return to Earth, but I do hope the ship will be able to ground me. If I lose my name [Alex, Fred], I hope the regression is not permanent. I know I can learn something from the bull, but maybe a bull can learn something from me, too. Identification is not intimidation after all. There's also love and reciprocity in it, or else it's all propaganda and indoctrination. If words don't make sense, I want to be able to eat them. Intellect that ignores appetite makes no sense that can guide you."

The first dream was reported in the seventh analytic session. In the preceding sessions Alex had talked and played, presenting himself basically as brash and defensive on the one hand and open and communicative on the other. Digging to the bottom of the sandbox, he commented, "I want to get to the bottom of things." He also hoped that the analyst would give him "the greatest memory in the world." All the meanings of this request would slowly emerge later in the analysis. He would build tall structures out of blocks of wood, reveling in the spatial majesty and in the destructive glee of toppling and dismantling. He would write his name on the blackboard and chalk in the number of times he had seen me, a somewhat arrogant "pupil" seizing as much control as possible from the "teacher" analyst.

I will present session seven in its entirety so that the dream and its context are fully exposed.

Alex entered the playroom, noticed that the block design from the previous session was not exactly as he had left it, and complained, "Why didn't you leave them up?"

ANALYST: You're angry that things are not exactly as you left them? [Pause] Could we make it again?
ALEX: No.
ANALYST: Oh?
ALEX: I can't remember. The mouse who takes things from the back of my head to the front...I can't get him to work now.

34

ANALYST: He's angry, too! He'd like things to stay in their place forever.

ALEX: Not forever. For one day!

ANALYST: [Touché—not voiced.]

ALEX: I'll make a bed. Pee-pee, doo-doo, wee-wee.

ANALYST: That's the way you talked when you were…how old?

ALEX: Three. I did pee-pee in bed last night.

ANALYST: Oh? How come?

ALEX: I wanted to.

ANALYST: Oh?

ALEX: To get Mommy to clean the sheet.

ANALYST: Oh, you get back at Mom that way?

ALEX: Yeah.

ANALYST: How did she get to you?

ALEX: She spanked me.

Alex suddenly climbed on the block shelves. I moved instinctively to protect him should he fall. (The shelves were tall given the size of the child.)

ALEX: Why did you move?

ANALYST: To make sure you were safely up.

ALEX: [Independently] I'm up now.

From his perch on the shelf, he erased his name and the number of sessions he had seen me from the blackboard, saying "Goodbye, Alex" to his name as it disappeared, and began to draw. "I want to draw a dog," he said, but instead he drew a dinosaur, a brontosaurus, and the bird dinosaur, saying, "The bird can eat the brontosaurus but not the tyrannosaur." Then he drew a lady snake and snake eggs and then a star, saying a star was a part of the night. "I don't like night."

ANALYST: Why not? Is it the dreams?
ALEX: Yes.
ANALYST: Last night?
ALEX: Yes.
ANALYST: What about?

Alex tells the following dream:

There was an octopus. As big as the Empire State Building. I had a stick. It swallowed me. I was fighting it. It spat me out.

ANALYST: It sounds scary.
ALEX: I had another dream about an octopus in a spook house.
ANALYST: What's a spook house?
ALEX: I don't know.
ANALYST: Sounds scary, too. Was it?
ALEX: Yeah.
ANALYST: Where do you think those dreams came from? Were you worried about something, maybe?
ALEX: Yeah, an accident.
ANALYST: Oh?
ALEX: Grandfather died. [This turns out to be a lie, but I am unaware of this at the time.]
ANALYST: Oh, I'm sorry to hear that. You miss him?
ALEX: Yeah and my uncle Abe.

Alex went to a drawer, extracted a hammer, and started to make a plane, cars, and a motorbike, tinkering away like a mechanic.

ANALYST: It feels good and strong to make things, especially when talking about scary dreams.

ALEX: [Went to the sandbox.] Let's bury Grandfather.

He spilled a lot of sand in the process, and I asked him to try not to, even if he was showing his feelings that way.

ALEX: I like to spill the sand.

ANALYST: Yes, you told me you like to mess and have someone else clean it up. Like a baby, I guess?

ALEX: I'd like to be a baby.

ANALYST: Oh? How come?

ALEX: I wouldn't have to eat roast beef and squash.

ANALYST: Oh? What would you prefer?

ALEX: Sol.

ANALYST: What's that?

ALEX: Soft baby food. I still like it.

[It's time to stop.]

ANALYST: Let's stop here.

ALEX: Oh, I'll take the airplane.

ANALYST: Can you leave it so we can use it again when we need to?

ALEX: Oh, but I want to paint it. [And he runs off with it.]

A Synopsis of the Psychoanalysis

The analysis brings to mind Ernest Jones's conviction that pathology of the phallic phase of development is intimately related to earlier disappointments at the breast. In other words, a phallus that "protests too much about its captivating seductiveness" is really a mouth in disguise, a mouth that did not possess the nipple adequately, and feeling dispossessed in one erotogenic zone tries to make up for it in another. Too much phallic pride, in other words, is a sign of oral disappointment.

Using the first dream as a guide to the initial transference communications, I believe Alex implied that his needs were urgent and even octopoid and that the little stick of his defenses might not be up to the task of taming so primitive an instinctual source unless an ally could be found in the analytic situation. There were many other meanings of the first dream, one could argue, but this particular transferential conceptualization highlighted the opening phase of analytic work and is being accentuated for that reason.

Two themes from the first year of analytic work seemed to grow like offshoots not only of the first dream but also of the story outlined in the anamnesis above. One theme developed into a play sequence where the analyst was Dr. Doolittle, the block shelf, which had wheels and could therefore "voyage" around the playroom, becoming a ship for Alexander and Dr. Doolittle to explore wild territories and "tame" all the wild animals. The other theme was closely related to this analytic investigation of Alexander's instincts and his struggles with control and compromise, adaptive expression, and symptomatic action. The voyage could get turbulent at times: the analyst got whacked on the head playfully with the broomstick oar on one occasion. But the voyage could be insightful and poignant as well. In one play sequence, the ship was actually compared to the analytic situation itself in a remarkable piece of insight for such a young child. When a toy ship was lost at sea and buffeted by storms but still managed to make it home safely to port, Alex interrupted the play for a moment and compared the work of analysis and the relationship he had with me to a voyage and a return trip to the safety and security of the analytic port, so to speak. Alex had returned the ship to the "terminal" and, turning to the analyst, said thoughtfully. "Maybe you can become a person terminal for me." The analyst was moved by Alex's suggestion of an emotional and psychological alliance between the young child and the analyst and commented genuinely on the remarkable understanding of the analytic process that the child appreciated at such a young age.

If Alex wished to fly and spit and swallow, he also hoped that there was a "vessel" somewhere that could contain him, hold him. In the final analysis, an analysand learned that the vessel was, of course, nothing other than one's own mind and its structures and instincts operating in that ironic harmony called conflict and compromise. In the course of the analytic journey one did not always feel that the mind was one's own as it leaned so desperately and so dependently into the deep paradox of transference that regressed it the better to strengthen it. At times the vessel seemed hopelessly lost at sea, and contact with another "human" vessel was mandatory if safe harbor was ever to be reached.

These two images of "taming" and "vessel" are not the only generative metaphors of a lengthy analysis, but they have an organizational focus that can be exploited in the interest of making a long analytic story short.

If Alex was frightened as well as exhilarated by forces that could dispatch analytic grandfathers—not to mention extra-analytic ones even closer to home—his skills at taming and vessel building were beginning to give him the confidence needed to pursue his analytic voyages no matter where they led. In child analysis, vessel building is not merely a metaphoric image: Alex actually carved boats out of wood, their meanings as variable as their contexts. For instance, a boat that he carved early in the analysis had quite a different meaning from the boat he carved at the end of the analysis. The first boat was carved in a context of exploration, which was complex and painful. The termination boat was more of a statement about journey's end than an exploration of any new unconscious territories. The first boat was called the *Catch Up,* and the termination boat could have been called the *Letting Go* but was, as will be disclosed later, given a more personal hieroglyphic code name as befits latency and all its developmental intrigue. The *Catch Up* was carved while Alexander was reviewing some complicated affects about a substitute caretaker Rosa, who left abruptly when Alexander was three, promising to return but never keeping her word. In a poignant moment when Alexander's phallic shield was lowered a little, he admitted that he took her at her word and counted the days to no avail. (Alex's numbering on the blackboard the sequence of days he had seen me could, with hindsight, now be seen in a more poignant, tragic light.) The loss of Rosa was made more traumatic by the even earlier emotional loss of mother. (The mother had confided in me that it was not in her nature to be close to Alex at bedtime, an emotional legacy that she inherited via the constricted affects of her own mother.) If the little bunny left home never to return, it was emotional retaliation, not first strike, it seemed in Alexander's primitive morality. But the *Catch Up* seemed to be an attempt to go beyond repetition compulsion and heal developmental wounds, not just rub them. Alex was trying to break a vicious cycle of neurosis in the mutative process of analysis: he was trying to replace neurotic convictions that warned (a) that loss of the object and its love would always cramp his phallic style; (b) that phallic disguise could always hide a broken heart (c) with the new conviction that would assure him that his libidinal expressiveness need not lead to such tragic consequences.

This new conviction was the offspring of several years of psychoanalytic work. Highlights of this process will give the gist if not the bulk of the analytic work over a few years. The latency years of the analysis were conducted in the typical climate of schoolboy psychology and defensiveness: an obsession with sports and other games hid the unconscious life of the mind with a developmental expertise that was impressive and, at times, impenetrable. However, in "scientific experiments" that were conducted by mixing detergents and other objects from every "primal" crevice of my office, affects were discussed and compared and contrasted according to their properties of speed or density. Anger, for instance, was an extremely fast affect, whereas sadness was extremely slow. Out of this alchemy of affects came the admission that the grief in the wake of Rosa's rejection was slow to leave him, the sadness lasting many months as he counted the days. Surely this was grief, a child's unique way of mourning (Mahon, 1977). Even the baseball resistance would occasionally surrender an unconscious meaning or two. Once in the middle of a baseball game with me, Alex complained that he had to interrupt the game to go to the bathroom, a deprivation that would not be necessary if the bathroom and the playroom were all one room instead of being separated. When I commented on how much Alex hated separations and interruptions, Alex said, "When the doodie goes out, the poopie goes up." Analysis of this cryptic comment in ensuing analytic sessions made it clear that what was said casually had quite deep levels of unconscious meaning. Since "doodie" was Alex's infantile word for feces and "poopie" his word for penis, his comment was a variation on Freud's penis = feces equation. In Alex's psychological calculus, when the doodie goes out, the poopie goes up meant: when you are faced with loss, you can cover your ass with an erect penis. The phallic boast attempts to hide the anal loss or the more deeply repressed oral loss. Penis = feces = breast, to complete Freud's equation.

Alex would often make insightful comments that suggested that even amid powerful defensive resistances, insight could emerge and take the analyst by surprise. A child analyst's ongoing commentary on the unfolding process is mostly informed by a defense analysis point of view. If the child is insisting that he is all-powerful like Batman, the analyst may say, "It must feel good to have Batman's kind of power when you're feeling weak after a hard day in school." If the child responds, saying, "Yes, today was awful; the teacher was mean to me all day," the analyst feels that his linking of defense and affect has been understood and insight has been advanced a little. Alex once commented on this analytic technique, saying, "You like to make things out of what I say." "Yes," the analyst says. "I guess I'm a different kind of teacher." "You sure are," Alex says, and the matter is dropped. The analyst realizes that Alex is developing some rudimentary idea of the interpretive process and how analysis works. In his own words, he seems to grasp what an interpretation tries to accomplish. On another occasion, when Alex was criticizing his parents' lack of empathy, he said, "Don't they know I need the person feelings?" This seemed like a profound insight, and the analyst was much moved by it. It seemed to refer again to the profound idea mentioned earlier in which Alex stepped out of the play about the ship in a storm getting home safely to the terminal and turning to the analyst and saying, "Maybe you can be a 'person terminal' for me." It is most arresting to hear a child's definition of the unique importance of what a 'person' signifies. He connects the 'person' with 'affect' in a most profound way. Sometimes the profound would emerge out of a game. Alex liked to play chess with the analyst. It was not chess in any formal sense but a version of chess in which the pieces could be moved in whatever manner the child's fantasies dictated. Once Alex picked up a pawn and asked, "Why can't a pawn become a king?" There was a poignancy in the wish as Alex identified with the pawn's role rather than with the king's role or with bishop's, knight's, rook's, or queen's. He could have identified with any piece, but the pawn's plight seemed to touch him the most and exposed his identification with the diminutive rather than with the high and mighty.

As Alex began to make remarkable progress on all fronts (social, academic, domestic, athletic) and termination began to make an impression on the clinical process, the baseball resistance reluctantly yielded a few important insights. When I interpreted the flurry of baseball resistances with a question, "Why so much baseball now that we're thinking of bringing our work to an end?" Alex replied, "Every baseball game has to end," proving that resistance is often an analyst's word for his own ignorance and that the analysand was in fact working on the termination phase in his play.

One of the final "symbols" of the analysis was the aforementioned boat, which might have been called the *Letting Go* but which was actually given a more phase-appropriate title by an industrious nine-year-old. Alex combined his own initials, my initials, and the numbers of our houses and street addresses into an impressive code name. At journey's end, the boats were left behind in the playroom to be retrieved perhaps in some future nostalgic catch-up or letting go. In the meantime, they remain among the treasured possessions of a nostalgic analyst.

This *Letting Go* boat was carved out of wood while many termination themes were being analyzed. Alex attempted to draw "a portrait of the analyst with a broken arm," in which his aggression toward the abandoning object could not be concealed. His anger at Rosa, his parents, his sister, and his analyst were worked over for many weeks. His fear in the face of all this aggression was that his hatred would destroy the object totally or at least the object's love for him. If he met Rosa in the street now, would he recognize her? Could he have a photograph of me to assure himself that his aggression had not destroyed all hope of ever seeing me again? Concerns such as these had to be broken into their genetic components (he felt like killing Rosa and his mother and father and feared that they would attack him or stop loving him or abandon him) before Alex could begin to realize that the past could be kept "in its place" and that the present could hold the promise of a future uncontaminated by the past.

The Second Dream

At age thirteen Alex returned for a consultation about the boarding school he would be attending soon. Boarding school was at least the manifest content of a visit that had obvious latent agendas as well, which could be addressed when he recounted a dream and began to work on it as if the

43

analysis had not ended at all! This immediacy of transference availability years after an analysis has terminated is well documented elsewhere, particularly in regard to adult analyses (Pfeffer, 1963).

The Dream

I am running in the woods. Snakes appear. They come close to my face. I run and run. There are other children younger than me playing nearby. I try to make the snakes go in their direction.

Alex's associations were of the superficial variety at first: he had watched a TV program on snakes, which explained their presence in the dream. The younger children referred to all the children that would be left in his school after he went off to boarding school. Then Alex went a little deeper: "close to his face" meant there was something dangerous he had to face—leaving home. Perhaps he was imagining the worst about boarding school. Was he seeing it as dangerous? Was he viewing it as punishment, being sent away? Was his "badness" catching up with him? Alex seemed relieved at airing some of these worries, affects, and distortions, but the dream seemed to be crying out for deeper exploration. Alex was now thirteen years old. He had grown a lot since I had seen him three years earlier. The transformations of puberty seemed to be waging a psychological civil war with the conservative forces of latency, and a developmental nudge in the form of an interpretation seemed appropriate. "What if the snakes represent your penis, which must have grown a lot like the rest of you?" I asked somewhat humorously. "Why do you suppose you'd be sending them away in the direction of younger children?"

Alex had no trouble getting the point. His immediate response was a confirmation of the interpretation in the form of a complaint: "My sister [two years older] didn't get her period until she was thirteen. I've had wet dreams and erections since I was eleven. It's not fair." Soon the irony of his own statement began to dawn on him. Here was the most "phallic" of boys suddenly renouncing his penis now that he was old enough to put it to use! This classical dilemma of the thirteen-year-old who finds progression and regression equally problematic was certainly not unique to Alex, but with five years of analysis behind him, it was easier for him to put words to his plight and recognize the deeply ambivalent psychological currents of his dream. Could he face the transformations of puberty? Could he acknowledge that his penis (snake) with its wet dreams and erections belonged to him and need not be delegated to others? Or would he invoke the personal myth of the deprived child whose older sibling had it easier? Even biology was kinder to her than to him, granting her a longer childhood, while he was expelled prematurely from the innocence of Eden by his hyperactive, precocious hormones! As Alex began to "play" with these associations, laughing at himself a good deal in the process, it became clear that his conflicts about sexuality, boarding school, and growing up were the "average expectables" of developmental life and not insurmountable obstacles that were about to derail him.

The Third Dream

Seven years passed before Alex consulted me again. By chance he had seen me on the street and recognized me, giving the lie to one of his termination fears (his anger would destroy the relationship; I would become unrecognizable). He was home from college, working as a cameraman's assistant on a movie being made not far from my office, when the chance encounter occurred. (Actually, I was unaware of the encounter until Alex told me later.)

The manifest reason for his visit was to discuss academic performance in college, which was reflecting his conflicts rather than his potential. But several more "latent" communications quickly came to the fore:

1. He had learned recently that Rosa's whole family had been killed in an auto accident. He was not sure whether Rosa herself had been killed or not.
2. A two-year relationship with a girlfriend had ended six months earlier: new relationships seemed ambivalent, tentative.
3. It was depressing to come home. His old room was now a storage room. His mother still seemed obsessed with herself and domestic details rather than with the emotional nuances of his development and conflicts.

We ran out of time on the first visit. We agreed to meet again, at which time Alex began the session with the following dream.

> I am in a Batmobile. Batman is driving. I'm in the back seat. The Batmobile is not all it's cracked up to be. We are trying to chase some bad guys. We are slow to pull out of the garage in pursuit because we have to make several broken U-turns just to get out of the driveway. Finally we get going. I take the wheel. Eventually we catch up with the bad guys. We follow them over a desert and give chase 'round and 'round an oval.

Alex had a wealth of associations to this dream. He had come into my office carrying a bicycle wheel, the rest of the bicycle locked to a tree outside for safekeeping. The bicycle wheel symbolized his return home to relative dependency. (In college he had a beaten-up used car and much more freedom.) He jokingly referred to this bicycle wheel as the Batmobile,

46

making it clear that vehicular symbolism was on his mind. He had a_lot of fun with the idea that the Batmobile in the dream was not the magical vehicle from the recent movie but a much more down-to-earth version. The broken U-turns were emblematic of his recent academic progress, which had been anything but linear in direction.

Alex had developed a capacity for laughing at himself, quite a contrast to the sensitivity and defensive bluster of his latency years. Alex's most emotionally laden associations were reserved for comparisons between the new "catch-up" vehicle (the Batmobile) and the old "catch-up" of yesteryear._It was in such a nostalgic moment that Alex referred to the automobile accident that claimed the lives of Rosa's family and maybe even Rosa herself. Alex's uncertainty about the fate of Rosa seemed highly significant. While she had not been a presence in his life for seventeen years, she had become symbolic of love, treachery, object constancy, transience—all the contrary motions of outer experience and inner psychology that left him confused at certain times, neurotic at others. Rosa was no longer a disappointing object out of the past: she had become a symbol of the internalized loving objects at the core of his self-esteem— one of the lynchpins that would determine the stability of his adolescent consolidations. In this context, it was clear to Alex that the Batmobile represented himself at the crossroads of his life. Batman was a reference to the idealized mother and father (Rosa too perhaps) who had to be diminished psychologically speaking if he was to assume the individuated responsibility for the wheel of his own life. (At this point in the hour the bicycle wheel leaning on the radiator beside Alex's chair assumed its full tragicomic significance!)

Chasing the bad guys around an oval led to several associations: the oval referred to the shape of the baseball field, "a field of dreams" he wished to return to and abdicate all adult ambition and conflict. In fact, in another dream fragment Alex reported, he_"surrenders" an old girlfriend to a rival while he in oedipal defeat becomes preoccupied with baseball. The pursuit of the bad guys leads to the most important association of all: Alex's realization that the bad guys are no longer out there as it seemed in latency times but within. Alex reflected on the fact that his academic progress was a very precise barometer of the state of his object relations. On reflection, he could see that the breakup of a two-year relationship with his girlfriend had affected him academically and emotionally more than he had been willing to admit prior to the consultation. There was no more time to pursue the analysis of the dream further. We left off with the idea that I was available should he want to consult me about his pattern of failed relationships with young women, his academic pursuits or any other issues, frivolous or serious, that he might want to discuss with me. He gave the overall impression of a young man seeking to find himself but not really ready to settle down quite yet into a totally stable identity.

The Fourth Dream

Infant falling out of plane. Plane escaping from aborigines. I look back in rearview mirror to catch a glimpse of infant if I can. I am copilot. Captain angry at me for looking back.

Alex was thirty years old when he reported this dream. He had returned briefly to discuss his relationships with women. He had continued to begin relationships fairly well but then lose out when the relationship got serious. He seemed restless and more interested in telling me about his bodybuilding regime than about the complexities of relationships. He had not really established himself yet as the skillful financial manager of a thriving firm he would eventually settle into. This was to be a short reengagement with psychoanalytic ideas before he vanished and maintained no further contact with me for twenty years. We did, however, spend a little time on the dream, which he described as alarming, given the image of the infant falling out of the plane with the plane proceeding as if nothing significant had happened. He had seen a movie about aborigines in Australia: he thought aborigine and infant were related. He believed that he was both captain and copilot and that the dream represented a conflict between his wish to be an infant and to be "flying high" at the same time. Before these issues could be explored in greater depth, Alexander broke off the contact with me, acting out the very symptom (conflict about commitment in a relationship) he had come to investigate. I would not see him again for twenty years.

The Fifth and Sixth Dreams

Alexander returned a few months before his fiftieth birthday. I was delighted and surprised to hear from him and to learn that he was happily married for seventeen years and had fifteen-year-old and thirteen-year-old sons. My surprise was a reflection of a countertransference fantasy in which he had concentrated on bodybuilding to the neglect of procreativity and object relations. I was thrilled that the predictive power of my magical countertransference bore no resemblance to reality whatsoever! Alex had started his own public relations company with a team of highly artistic, business-savvy colleagues, a cutting-edge enterprise that had flourished and had satellite national and international offices. But success phobia became a feature of Alex's career and lifestyle. His wife had suggested that he call me since he had been staying out late with his young employees, who would go out drinking in the evenings when the workday had ended. Alexander never had any interest in alcohol, but he envied the camaraderie his younger colleagues enjoyed so much as they relaxed in local saloons when the workday ended. When he discussed this behavior with his wife, Alexander sensed it was the fear of turning fifty that had triggered the regression and prompted a kind of infantile behavior fueled by a fantasy that he was still in his thirties and not approaching fifty at all. Alexander would grow bored of the inebriated conversations, as he remained sober while his colleagues regressed, and yet he felt drawn to these evening get-togethers despite his sense that he was enacting a symptom rather than analyzing it. The couple had been married for seventeen years, and it was a good relationship that he would hate to compromise based on a return to behavior that "was beneath his status," as his wife put it. Alexander agreed to meet regularly and try to understand what the unconscious mischief was all about. He expressed the opinion that it should not take too long to understand this behavior and repudiate it.

Alexander reported two dreams not long after we had decided to work together again.

The Fifth Dream

I am wearing a white shirt. There is blue sticking tape attached to it. I try to remove it but cannot seem to pry it successfully off the shirt.

We had been talking about his reaction to turning fifty, and when I suggested that in the dream he was attempting perhaps to rid himself of the aging process, he agreed and said, "And I'm blue about it." And then told a second dream he remembered.

The Sixth Dream

With Jared Kushner's brother. He has information about a real estate deal Trump is involved in. This information can help Trump.

So we meet Trump on a football field. The dreamer (Alexander) is looking up to/at him.

Alexander had many associations to this dream, mostly about size and stature. Trump is six feet, three inches. Melania is five feet, eleven inches. Their son, Baron, is tall. By contrast, Alexander is only five feet, nine inches. His wife and sons are also short. Alexander wishes his sons were taller than he. The football field refers to Trump being actually on a football field recently, celebrating a college football game. Alexander felt ambivalent about looking up at Trump. In terms of the economy and taxes, the country was doing well. But there was no question that Trump was "a black eye on the face of America." And yet he was looking up at him. "That's not the same as looking up *to* him," he suggested. And so he changed the subject to his hanging out with inebriated subordinates. He socialized with his staff, who were all younger than he. He believed he was blurring the distinction between the "boss" and his underlings. He felt uncomfortable at the top.

When I asked Alexander if he remembered any of the dreams he had told me years earlier, he said he could not recall working on them. He did remember the boats we had made together, the *Catch-Up* and the *Letting Go*. When I told him about his dream at age twelve, he could not remember it but reminded me of a dream he had at age thirteen about a fire engine. He was able to date it to age thirteen because the family had been vacationing at the time in a certain hotel and he associated the dream with the hotel. And he remembered telling the dream to me.

The Seventh Dream

I am driving a fire engine. Not the front steering wheel but the one in the back of the vehicle. I am having trouble steering and coordinating with the main driver.

Alexander agreed that there seemed to be a theme that linked that dream with his current concerns about steering his company or his family as the number one guy who is comfortable with authority.

Development and continuity are strikingly etched in a study such as this. Mind and body go through extraordinary developmental changes from birth to eighteen years of age. From eighteen years on there may be subtle developmental changes also, but these have not been codified as much, if at all. If one looks at development through a Piagetian lens alone, the evolution of sensorimotor, pre-operational, operational, and formal cognitive masteries is a marvel to behold. The advance from preconceptual to conceptual to hypothetico-deductive, formal adolescent reasoning is a fifteen-year achievement almost too challenging to fathom. Imagined with time-lapse photography, this sweep of human developmental change is a miracle on the move. Seen through a Freudian lens alone, the sweep of sexual and assertive/aggressive incremental change from incipient attachment to separation individuation, to adaptive engagement with oedipal conflict, to the sudden arrival of an infantile amnesia that represses the first six years of memory almost in its entirety, to the intellectual industry of latency that allows the mind to be schooled in and to slowly imbibe the fruits of cultural input; and on to the intellectual pyrotechnics of adolescent thought, which allows free-associative mastery to be achieved, is staggeringly impressive. That said, while there are these incremental changes in structure and content, there is also a continuity of psychological themes that becomes highlighted in a longitudinal study such as this. And it is this balance between developmental change and tenacious continuity that I wish to highlight.

In a sense, the stubborn insistence of continuity and the incremental changes of development could be recognized as the overdetermined vicissitudes of long-term psychological conflict that will never be *completely resolved, except* in adaptive compromise. The mind remains a political theater of opposing forces throughout life: it was Hartmann, I believe, who suggested this political metaphor, but the idea of ongoing psychological conflict has always been the core idea of psychoanalysis since its inception. Development assists the mind in its struggles with conflict from dyadic pre-oedipal separation-individuation issues to triadic oedipal turmoil. Freud's theory of a "dissolution" of the Oedipus complex at age six as the newly structured mind authorizes the superego to squash oedipal desires in the interest of civil obedience had to be modified. The Oedipus complex is not squashed. There is no absolute dissolution. There is repression, to be sure, and identification with authority rather than anarchic perpetual strife with it. There is sublimation of hatred rather than chronic enactment of it. The infantile amnesia that lowers its curtain, at age six approximately, on the whole tormented sexuality and aggression of pre-oedipal and oedipal drama is remarkable to witness as parent or analyst as latency transforms a wild imaginative preconceptual animistic child into a reasoning conceptual being who embraces the intellectual challenges of a world of "reading, writing, and arithmetic" with an industry that is impressive, as Erikson noted.

In this discussion I will compare and contrast developmental change and the seemingly unchanging continuity of the earliest desires of infancy, early childhood, latency, adolescence, young adulthood, adulthood proper. Continuity is not static, of course. It is always being challenged and modified by the developing mind's maturing structures and sophistications of defense. The metaphors at the mind's disposal will change from octopus and sticks to snakes and bicycle wheels, to fire engines and Batmobiles, to airplanes with infants falling out of them, to a dreamer looking up at/ to Trump. Each developmental epoch, be it pre-oedipal, oedipal, latency, adolescence, young adulthood, middle age, old age, will deal with conflict uniquely, differentially, and yet the continuity of the desire to be taller, to be more phallic (which may of course be a poignant cover-up of a deeper longing to be held and cherished by a "person terminal" that represents mother/father/Rosa/wife/analyst) will persist. The great psychological theater that illustrates these developmental lurches and abiding continuities is the transference/countertransference drama that dyadic analysis exploits as it proceeds on its therapeutic odysseys.

The Complexities of Transference/Countertransference Issues

It is strange to be analyzing a man at age fifty that you analyzed already at four or five years of age. It is strange to be in possession of knowledge that the previous child analysis yielded, knowledge that the current analysand knows only partially or unconsciously. It is akin to Freud's astonishment when Herbert Graf returned to see the professor who conducted an analysis via the father that Little Hans, now age nineteen, had no memory of all the extraordinary, even revolutionary ideas that that analysis had uncovered, now returned to the unconscious from whence they had first sprung! For instance, when the analyst shared with Alexander his dreams from age four and thirteen, Alexander, not unlike Herbert Graf, did not remember them even though he did remember the wooden boats he had carved and painted in the company of his analyst when he was six and eight years old. While he did not remember the second dream I have outlined above, he did remember an alternate dream he recalled from that same period when he was twelve years old. It is clear that selective memory, repression, infantile amnesia are in evidence in what Alexander recalls and does not recall.

I have used the word "strange" twice in the last paragraph, and it cries out for analysis of the countertransferential complexity compressed in it. The most accessible countertransferential affect consciously available to me is a sense of pride, pleasure, joy that I was fortunate enough to be in the position to receive dreams such as these over such a long span of time.

Since the whole engagement with the dreamer was not planned in any way except for the years of the child analysis, all subsequent unpredictable visits seemed fortuitous, almost uncanny. But the affect on seeing an old patient return on four subsequent occasions bearing dreams did seem *strange*, to use that vague language again. There was a magical sense that this long clinical follow-up could go on providing research data about development and the evolution of the dreaming process forever. Mortality and transience were surely being denied here. Since I had heard Paul Dudley White (many years ago, when internal medicine was my first choice of a career) speak about the endless information regarding the natural course of normality and pathology that the long clinical follow-up could provide the curious, scientific practitioner, I had imagined that psychoanalysis was surely the epitome of the long clinical follow-up, the human mind itself on display for the analytic dyad to explore endlessly. The word "endlessly" exposes the countertransference embedded in the fantasy of the long clinical follow-up, as if the history of ideas could be the sole property of any one observer as opposed to the legacy of all scientists over time. That particular countertransference also ignores the goal of the essential function of analysis, which is to restore the analysand to the management of his own individuality (Poland, 2015) once the work of analysis has achieved its goals. Analysis was not meant to be interminable, no matter what countertransference insists or claims to the contrary!

Child analysis breeds its own particular kind of countertransference perhaps, given that the analyst becomes such a real object in the child's mind. This is surely true in adult analysis as well, but in adult analysis the very nature of the relationship between analyst and analysand becomes one of the great windows into the elucidation of the whole analytic process as the transference/countertransference relationship is explored in depth constantly. In child analysis the real relationship between the child and analyst is *experienced* rather than constantly explored or deconstructed.

This is a relative issue to be sure and worthy of deeper commentary. One of the dangers of countertransference in child analysis is its cultivation of a neurotic proprietary sense that views the child as the analyst's child even when the child is fifty years old! I believe I have guarded against this pitfall by insisting on its becoming conscious rather than remaining unconscious. The corollary of this is equally important: the fifty-year-old man may wish to remain a child in the analyst's eyes forever. The dream in which Alex is looking at/up to Trump highlights this issue. Is Alex trying to draw attention to his need to analyze the profound difference between looking *up at* someone as opposed to looking *up to* someone? Looking up *at* someone is merely a spatial issue; looking up *to* someone is an emotional/psychological issue. Alex's shorter size makes him look up at people taller than he. But he does not need to look *up* to them unless he truly admires them in a nonneurotic evaluation. This issue was just being explored when Alex needed to interrupt our work based on a worldwide financial crisis. There may have been a resistance issue as well, of course. It is possible that Alex felt the need to assert his individuated status rather than surrender it to an analyst he still looks up to too much, thereby weakening and diminishing his own status. (It is possible that this may be explored analytically in future sessions, but for the present such analysis must be postponed.)

Could all of Alex's return visits to the person terminal be viewed as bouts of refueling, a concept Margaret Mahler used to describe the behavior of the child in the rapprochement period of development when the eighteen-month-old is testing the wings of individuation by making more and more excursions away from the mother, while at the same time retracing the footsteps to the source to make sure that the journey away can always be undone, confirming over and over that love is not lost as separateness and individuality are being experimented with and gradually established. At eighteen months this doing and undoing in action becomes the precursory model of the later psychological doings and undoings that typify the defensive, more intrapsychic aspects of such psychodynamics. Is Alex *refueling* as he returns to the person terminal, and can it be analyzed as such so that its psychological dimensions can be deconstructed and the repetitive nature understood so well that it becomes unnecessary? Is that how the analysand will terminate from the person terminal when such issues are completely metabolized? Such questions may perhaps be answerable in future visits either to this analyst or to a new analyst. Countertransference must be willing to contemplate the retirement or demise of the analyst and how the work might proceed with a new person terminal.

Development and Continuity

From a developmental point of view, Alex's goals could be depicted as a voyage through the pre-oedipal and oedipal complexities of the first six years of life into the relatively smoother waters of latency and then through the rapids of adolescent turmoil into the challenges of adulthood. The first dream suggests just how complex this voyage is going to be. Each image of the dream is fraught with the combustible nature of instinctual unconscious life. *There is an octopus. As big as the Empire State Building. I had a stick. It (the octopus) swallowed me. I was fighting it. It spat me out.*

If every image of this dream represents a facet of Alex's unconscious mind as it struggles to represent its conflicts, the octopus is perhaps the most striking and overdetermined. Surely it could represent the desire of this most phallic boy to have eight penises as opposed to just one endangered organ. His symptomatic behavior in school, grabbing at the penises of other boys, represents the frantic nature of this kind of endangered interiority, not to mention inferiority. But, of course, the octopus is a devouring creature and may well represent Alex's hunger for love, sympathy, contact, nourishment as well as a more primitive desire to sink his teeth into the breast of this world and be loved for all his aggression. The Empire State Building looms large in his ideals and introduces the concept of size that will be such a dominant psychological motif throughout his symphonic development. His little stick represents a more accurate view of his diminutive anatomical size perhaps and how his normal phallic-oedipal strivings can be swallowed so readily by the regressive overwhelming pre-oedipal oral longings that have never been adequately engaged by a facilitating environment that allowed its own past conflicts with unfinished parental development to interfere with parenting in the present. This was an intergenerational transmission of neurosis that had a significant effect on Alexander. The mother's understanding of her own conflicts without being able to correct them as they engaged with Alex's development became, nevertheless, an important affective co-operative corroboration and endorsement of the analytic enterprise that nourished Alex's development, albeit indirectly. Child analysis cannot proceed to a beneficial outcome without such cooperation from sympathetic parents. The analyst's skill in maintaining a strong alliance with the parents is crucial as the storms of the child analytic process are being negotiated. Child analyses are often interrupted or scuttled by parents who become envious rivals of the analytic process rather than supporters of it. It is the analyst's responsibility to be attuned with parental attitudes throughout the process.

The octopus has a transferential meaning, of course, as the first dream image to capture the nascent relationship between the tall person terminal and the diminutive boy at the beginning of what surely must seem to him to be an adventure into wonderland with a giant! And what a strange giant his imagination dreams up! An octopus as big as the Empire State Building! Anatomy makes it impossible for him not to look *up* at this giant analyst. Hope will insist that the giant should be a person terminal he can look *up to*. From whatever angle one studies these first unconscious moves in the incipient analytic chess game, it is the transference and its myriad potentials that will steer the imagination throughout the process. Alex's initial transference fantasy suggests that as a very little boy it is best to carry a stick and hope that your phallic aspirations can guide you through the looming fantasies of the curious analytic journey ahead.

The relative dissolution of the Oedipus complex is negotiated at approximately age six, when the infantile amnesia shelves the bulk of the affective storms the first six years of developmental life struggled with. Latency then ushers in a new kind of engagement with those earlier conflicts. Psychodynamic and developmental components make this extraordinary transition possible. Identification with the parental authorities that had been challenged so vigorously up until now brings about a developmental détente. Repression seals the deal, so to speak. Sublimation and all the other defensive maneuvers have roles to play in paving the way for latency to become consolidated. Alex from age six to nine engages in analytic process that is decidedly more controlled by ego growth and defensive achievements. One aspect of countertransference in child analysis is the analyst's regret that the imaginative playful dramatic elements of prelatency analytic process have been transformed into much tamer expressions of themselves. The analyst must recognize that the advance into latency is a triumph of developmental progression and not some less poetic version of the child that latency has produced. It is the cognitive, conceptual advances of the child's more mature ego that assist the child in his struggle with oedipal impasse by convincing him that his phallic equipment is numerically the equivalent of his parent's. Perceptual size no longer trumps numerical conceptual abstraction in the brave new Piagetian world of the concrete operations of latency (Mahon, 1990). Boy and man, son and father have one penis despite the size difference. That Alex has not completely metabolized this concept is a demonstration of how neurosis can continue to compromise cognitive conceptual achievement no matter how advanced in age you are!

It is striking how whenever Alex returns to the analytic setting, whether at twelve or nineteen or thirty or fifty, he immediately reacts as if no time has passed at all and the analytic relationship proceeds again without much sense of the significant gaps that occurred between nine and fifty. Alex may not remember all the psychological links of the analytic process, but the trust in and reliability of the relationship (with the person terminal) seems a constant. He tells dreams as if that is natural and comes with the territory. At fifty he knows that the two dreams are significant and he is willing to work on them; in addition, he remembers a dream from age thirteen even if he doesn't remember the other dreams from ages four, twelve, and nineteen. He is aware that turning fifty has great emotional and psychological significance for him, and he associates freely to the images in the dreams.

Size was one of the first issues in the manifest content of his dreams that seemed pivotal in Alex's endangered psychology since he first introduced the octopus to be as *big* as the Empire State Building in the first dream. Alex had only a small stick to defend himself with. The architectural size of the octopus and the diminutive size of the stick are poignantly striking. In the Trump dream, size seems to be significant again. Trump is tall, as are his wife and son. By contrast, Alex and his wife and son are all short. Alex is aware that having to look up at a taller person is not the same as looking up *to* someone, which implies admiration, idealization, or respect. He knows that Trump is an embarrassing national disgrace, "a black eye on the face of America," as he put it. Given how important the economy was in Alex's line of business, his ambivalence was understandable even though it troubled him greatly. Size and value are quite different entities, and yet Alex's old conflicts about his vulnerable size and status in the precarious unconscious world relied on magical thinking to sustain them.

Even turning fifty could be seen as an issue of size and stature: It was as if age diminished your size. It was a blue adhesion to your shirt that could never be removed. It brought depression (the blues) with it, and it could never be undone since age could never be reversed. It was best to fall in line with the Kushners of this world, feed the information to the tall man and hope that some of the tallness would rub off on you.

The latent dream thoughts in the Trump dream that the dream-work transformed into the manifest imagery reflected Alex's conflicts about size. Alex, despite his short stature, has information in the dream that can help the taller Trump. As a statement of transference, this could be read as the analysand believing that he has inside (unconscious) information that will be useful to divulge to the tall analyst. Now, while it is true that every analysand has the insider information in his unconscious mind that can break the pathological code that has compromised his development, it is important that the analysand realizes that analysis is a collaborative project. The analysand does not just hand the information over to the idealized person terminal. He also collaborates with the analyst in a mutual voyage of discovery. Alex has looked up to the person terminal identity of the analyst since he was a child. But that does not mean the relationship with the analyst is devoid of conflict. In the manifest content and in the first associations to the dream, Trump and his wife and son are admirably tall. He looks up at Trump even if he does not want to look up to him. But there is an unconscious wish not to look up to anyone but to be secure in one's own skin. Trump as a black eye on the face of America is relevant in this context. The imagery is revealing. A black eye suggests violence: someone has blackened Trump's eye. Alex may need to look up at him, but he also wants to give him a black eye. Alex once hit the child analyst with a broomstick when they were playing the Dr. Doolittle voyages to tame the wild animals. Even when the mission is to tame the wild, the wild may still feel compelled to lash out at the doctor, who does little to calm the wild instinctual states Alex needs to tame in the company of his person terminal.

This is the ambivalence that all analyzes engage with as positive and negative oedipal transferences display themselves in the analytic process. As an association to the size issue in the Trump dream, Alex expressed the wish that his sons would grow taller than he. Oedipal desire has been reversed in this association. Alex wants the best for his sons to be sure, but in normal development the father doesn't have to diminish his own size to masochistically enhance the stature of his sons. In child analysis, when the analyst and analysand were playing chess, Alex bemoaned the fact that the pawn could not just assume the size of the king and win the game readily. This poignant oedipal wish is still reflected in Alex's associations to the Trump dream. Analysis tries to change a perpetual idealization that looks up to the person terminal without ever valuing self-regard, self-sufficiency, and agency adequately.

Neurosis could be defined as a pawn that forever yearns to possess the stature of the king without realizing that both sides of a chessboard come with equal chess pieces and that he is in possession of a king already and does not need to yearn for one. Alex has not resolved this essential oedipal conflict without resorting to self-diminishing tactics. His current resolution seems to need socialization with inebriated subordinates to blur the oedipal distinction between him and his employees. It also needs the fantasy of sons growing taller than their father. Alex's reliance on the concept of a person terminal needs to be able to incorporate the idea that in a healthy object relationship, no party lords their stature over another. Mature love is not perpetual dependence looking up to the need-satisfying object obligatorily but an insistence on equal status that has integrated love and aggression into its philosophy. Both parties to such mature love are equally assertive. Neither has more stature than the other nor would think of claiming it.

The dream that Alex remembered from age thirteen about the fire engine and the two drivers front and back with Alex in the back having trouble steering the vehicle had an oedipal core to it that was as prominent at fifty as it was at thirteen. In early adolescence the two dreams are very revealing. The dream about Alex sending the snakes away toward the younger children shows how ironic the phallic defense was: Alex liked to strut his cockiness, but when adolescence presented him with the potential for actual sexual prowess, he felt completely overwhelmed by such developmental precocity and ambition. Why was this developmental stature being thrust upon him so prematurely? His sister had not been rushed into her developmental maturity prematurely. There is something poignant about this dream that wishes to throw the oedipal stick (penis) away and stay swallowed by the pre-oedipal primitive octopus (womb?) and remain infantile forever. Similarly, the fire-engine dream highlights Alex's wish to be second fiddle, and even as second fiddle, the developing fiddle doesn't seem to work properly. This type of conflict resolution seems to be displayed in Alex's character. (He sometimes acts as if he were not the co-owner of his own business but a subordinate looking up at superiors rather than sharing the crown with them.) This lessening of his status is ego syntonic for Alex: It is displayed in the symptom that brought him back into treatment: his hanging out with his inebriated subordinates blurs the distinction between his status and theirs. Such neurotic behavior also demeans him in the eyes of his wife and sons. Alex abhors this symptomatic behavior consciously but unconsciously seems to rely on its regressive energies.

If size (as a reflection of self-esteem and oedipal prowess) is a prominent manifest dream issue, another theme that could be isolated for closer scrutiny is "vessel," whether it be boat or fire engine or Batmobile or airplane. The fire-engine dream from age twelve, which he reported at age fifty, is the first iteration perhaps of being second-in-command as a resolution of oedipal strivings. The dream of snakes close to his face that he wishes to send away toward younger children complements that neurotic solution. In the fire-engine dream, Alex is driving the rear wheel of the fire engine and not very competently. Being second fiddle seems not to be enough of a regression: incompetence reverses the assertive oedipal desire even more so. What is striking, of course, is the timing of these dreams to coincide with the onset of adolescence and its sexual and ambitious awakenings. Similarly, the Batmobile dream seems to reflect a lack of readiness for mature age-appropriate action. And the airplane dream from age thirty seems to be a continuation of the theme. Alex is copilot (second-in-command) and reprimanded by the head pilot for giving his attention to an infant that had fallen out of the plane. The conflict between pre-oedipal dependency needs and more assertive oedipal needs seems to be illustrated by this manifest imagery. It is striking that vessels in manifest dream content are a reflection of conflicted ambivalent ambition, whereas the actual vessels (boats) that Alex carved and painted while in child analysis seemed much more progressive rather than regressive. The Dr. Doolittle voyages on the "bookshelves boat" were excursions into the wild in the service of taming it and changing wild instincts into adaptive social communications. Another boat (the *Catch-Up*) was designed to help him propel his analysis forward, and yet another (the *Letting Go*) was designed to help him terminate. The portrait of the analyst with a broken arm contained and expressed the aggression he felt about graduation from analysis, but the *Letting Go* boat was a concrete substitute for the person terminal he must now take his leave of. By carving initials and addresses into the sides of the boat, he was perpetuating the contact with his person terminal, in fantasy to be sure, but fantasy framed in the concrete reality of a piece of sculpted art.

While it could be argued that the first three dreams suggest ways of thinking about development from four to nineteen and how unconscious infantile wishes react to and reflect different developmental challenges as prelatency becomes latency and latency becomes adolescence, all the dreams from four to fifty could be thought of as a seamless flow of unconscious infantile wishes modified, to be sure, by fast-changing developmental experiences. In other words, there is a continuity of desire, ambition, disappointment, aggression that persists throughout life even if development, in the first eighteen years of that life, changes the cognitive and psychological equipment that shapes the expression as life proceeds. Development and continuity can clash. Maturation and development proceed whether the ego is ready for it or not. Alex's phallic erections were experienced as developmental challenges that he was not ready for. This unreadiness acts like a day's residue that becomes one ingredient in the formation of the dream. If development itself is a theme, the theme of size and stature as well as the wish to attain a personhood that is cherished and promoted by parents and substitute "person terminals," is a lifelong project that analysis and post-analytic self-analysis must always engage with.

Alex invoked the concept of a person terminal early in his child analysis. It is a generative concept that will change and mature over time as it engages conflict throughout life. A person terminal not only survives the analysand's aggression but welcomes it so that the analysand knows through an analytic sustained experience that his fight with the unconscious octopus will clear the necessary space for octopus and stick-wielding child to cohabit in the democracy of the unconscious, in the united states of a fully integrated psyche. A fully integrated psyche must, of course, contend with oedipal as well as pre-oedipal development. Alex's current resolution of oedipal conflict is a compromise formation that is adaptive in many ways but diminishing and maladaptive in others. The need to hang out with inebriated employees of lesser stature than himself exposes his fear of fully claiming his own full stature. But if this is an obligatory lessening of his stature in the service of neurosis, a basic retreat from full engagement with the Oedipus complex, it may weaken his self-image in a chronically demeaning, fearful manner. He shouldn't be *obliged* to look up to leaders rather than claiming that honor for himself. He shouldn't need his sons to be taller than he based on an unconscious fear of being a powerful father and claiming that loving assertive authority for himself. He needs to become a fully integrated person terminal, secure in his own authority to define what personhood is when it completely strips itself of any mind-forged manacles.

I would like to end with a discussion of a final countertransferential attitude. Alex may have gotten what he wanted, or certainly what he needed, to gain victory over a symptom that was compromising his relationship with his wife and sons. Should the analyst be satisfied that the consumer has returned to refuel with the person terminal and after sufficient engagement with the analyst has set his life on the proper course again? In this vision of development, Alexander has accomplished his immediate goal and may never return for further analysis. His self-analyzing instrument, fashioned over the years by his collaborative work with the analyst, has kicked in, and now he wishes to steer the vessel of his life alone. The analyst would surely be content with this outcome unless there were some nagging unanswerables tugging at the sleeve of his own unconscious deliberations. Did Alexander sense that the analyst was a much older person terminal than the original boat builder? Could he paint a portrait of this older person terminal with a broken arm, and would such aggression be as welcome today as it was in the past? Did Alexander leave prematurely, exploiting a world financial crisis as a most convenient resistance to the full exploration of such issues? This is all countertransferential speculation since no such issues were explored in the sessions I have described earlier. Alexander would have to return at some point in the future before such issues could be addressed. Perhaps it is neurotic to emphasize such countertransference naggings as if some hunger for further knowledge from the unconscious trove that Alexander's dream life exhibits makes one lose sight of what the collaborative psychoanalytic labor has accomplished already.

3
DREAMS WITHIN DREAMS

The concept of a dream within a dream is fascinating. If dreams are uncanny by definition when they seem to employ a kind of oneiric mitosis to bamboozle the dream censor even further, then the weird experience of a dream within a dream is born! The illusion created by the dream-work portrays one portion of the dream enacted within the envelope of the other. Freud (1900) emphasized that the function of placing a piece of reality in a dream within a dream is an attempt to rob it of its significance and obliterate it. However, he seemed curiously disinterested in the fact that segmentation of a dream text into two seemingly discrete fragments does offer a dream investigator the opportunity to explore the dynamic relationship between the two fragments and the multiple meanings of the illusion created during sleep. In this study, the linkage between the two parts of the dream sequence is highlighted. While Freud's intuition is corroborated, his lack of interest in the duality of the dream events is puzzling, as if he believed that only the dream *within* the other dream was meaningful and the other "containing" dream could be ignored. In this section of this chapter I suggest that both portions of a dream within a dream are significant, the one helping to explicate the other as the free-associative process of dream interpretation gives equal democratic time to both.

I pose the following question: Why would a dreamer immersed in the illusion of dream imagine he has awakened but in fact go on dreaming a "new dream" so that on actual awakening his experience will seem to have been that he has had a dream within a dream? If one pictures a dream within a dream cinematically and if it is possible to retrieve the unconscious moment that signals the end of reel one and the activation of reel two, so to speak, what unique unconscious psychology could account for this cinematographic decision?

The topic was first introduced by Sigmund Freud in 1900 and since then has received surprisingly scant attention, Berman and Silber being notable exceptions. Whether this means that the phenomenon is rare or simply underreported is not clear.

Freud in 1900 insisted that a dream within a dream was a sure sign that something that had actually happened was being disavowed vehemently. "If a particular event is inserted into a dream...by the dream-work itself, this implies the most decided confirmation of the reality of the event." To place a dream within the envelope of another dream suggested that a reality was being hidden with such precision that an astute awakener would raise his eyebrows at the elaborate mechanism of disguise.

My goal in this chapter is not only to reexamine Freud's thesis but also to address his neglect of the envelope as he focused solely on its contents. In other words, I will argue that a dream within a dream has two dream portions, one seemingly housed in the other, that both portions are part of one elaborate illusion and that both can be studied profitably.

One assumption of this segment of our dream exploration is that a "formal" retextualization of the unfolding screenplay of a dream must be in response to the emergence in the dream state of affect that cannot be disguised with the "usual" primary processes (condensation, displacement, symbolism) but requires a fundamental relocation of the drama to resolve or at least manage the conflict and keep the dreamer asleep. That is, reels are switched dramatically for urgent dynamic reasons.

The dream within a dream that is scrutinized here occurred in the eighth year of an analysis, a clinical context that allowed the topic to be viewed through the lens of a complex transference neurosis. Genetics, dynamics, transference, and countertransference had been explicated again and again so that termination was now the focus and perhaps one of the main triggers of the dream.

The dreamer is fifty-six years old, French by birth, an ex-priest, a professor of philosophy, recently married, with one child. The analysis could be portrayed as the deconstruction of a conscience so jesuitical in its brilliant mixture of menace, mischief, and multiple ambiguities as to be almost unreachable, its mental quicksilver visible, touchable, but hard to pick up or hold on to.

The dream was reported as follows:

I awake at the sound of a car pulling into the driveway of our Connecticut house. It is pitch-dark, but a child is being dropped off as if our home were a nursery school. All this seemed natural in dream experience even though the time, the darkness, would have been highly unusual for such a drop-off in real time. The scene shifts. I am now outside my house but lost, trying to find my bearings. A child on a bicycle guides me home. Then I walk from my house in Connecticut to Greenwich Village, which in dream geography seems no more than a hundred yards. I am so surprised by the spatial novelty of Connecticut's being a stone's throw from Greenwich Village that I wake up—an illusion, as I will discover on actual awakening. In Greenwich Village, I walk into a wood-lined office in a town house. A bearded man, not unlike the young Freud in the Freud-Fliess era, greets me. I start to tell him the unusual dream I've just had about being lost and how it was a child who guided me home.

When the dreamer awakens, he begins to tell his wife the dream immediately, and while recounting the dream, he has a déjà phenomenon, as if he had told her the dream already. He is aware that the dream-within-a-dream phenomenon of telling the dream to the bearded man in Greenwich Village is what gives the déjà experience with his wife such an uncanny feeling. (A dream followed by a déjà feeling is noteworthy, in and of itself: it suggests that the magical thinking of dream time spilled over into immediate post-dream experience, night refusing to accept, too readily, the terms daylight insists on imposing.) The associations were genetic, dynamic, freely flowing, and far ranging. New insights were generated as dream, and dream within dream were examined for several weeks. The theme of a lost childhood as well as an actual experience of being lost at age five had been analyzed from various angles over the years. But the dream-within-a-dream treatment of it seemed to generate new affects, more intense memory. The analysand, whose reading of Freud was deep and well integrated into his overall philosophical knowledge (a factor that could be a resistance at times but often was a promoter of insight), was not unaware of Freud's contributions to the topic. "One hides in a dream within a dream an actual event," he commented, paraphrasing Freud. "In that case, depending on which of the dreams is within the other, being lost could be the disavowed actuality, or is it 'telling' about it that is the significant reality that is being relegated to dream life, doubly displaced and captioned as non-real in its dream-within-dream status?" Several questions had been raised that would take time to address. If there was no new "topic" at this stage of analysis, the same could not be said of affect. Memory and history were not files in an unconscious library but sudden revelations of the self in a living mirror that could surprise and astonish no matter how clever the defensive anticipations. Which part of the dream was within the other? If the totality of the dream is looked upon as one text, the illusion of waking up and telling the dream to a bearded man in Greenwich Village would seem to be the part of the dream that is within the other, larger, earlier part. However, looking at the dream as a total text, one could argue that the first part is being told again in the later dream and is therefore "within" it, making the analysand's question not as "intellectual" as it seemed at first blush. This raises the question of whether the two dream pieces can be studied in isolation or separately, a task Silber (1983) set himself in his brilliant paper on the topic, no doubt to keep his focus scientific and uncluttered.

Which actuality was being disguised, the experience of being lost or the telling about it? This led to a series of intriguing sessions, but some genetic context must be described to make the narrative intelligible.

Mr. Perdu (a fictitious name for the analysand) had recounted early in his analysis how once as a child in the South of France he had been playing with older boys who suddenly went about their own business, forgetting the younger one, who'd been entrusted to their care. He imagines he was five or six in the memory. A kind gentleman on a bicycle rode him home to his house. In later years, whenever this incident was recalled, his mother would rail against the boy to whom she had entrusted her son, taking little responsibility for her own negligence. "Quel salot," she would scream, blaming the boy for her own delinquency. Mr. Perdu was aware that in the dream "a child on a bicycle who guided him home" was a reversal of the actual roles of child and adult fifty years before the dream. This childhood memory had been analyzed intensely, but the reversal and the elaborate dream-work that dream-within-dream implied suggested, as Freud would have argued, that this was the reality whose disavowal in dream-within-dream was in fact a powerful affirmation of its significance.

Mr. Perdu, an only child, had for years insisted that a great closeness had existed between him and his mother—an assertion that memory and dream seemed to challenge. His father's alcoholism and fiscal irresponsibility left the family in dire straits often, until the mother started her own business and essentially became the breadwinner. He idealized the mother's resourcefulness and courage and could not remember ever feeling any anger toward her. The anger he felt toward his father could not be expressed, either, except in pity and shame. A vicious superego became the heir of these unspeakable hatreds for years, quite ego syntonic with the vicious Catholic God Mr. Perdu had enshrined in the Vatican of his mind throughout his pre-analytic existence. But an unconscious rebel was there, too, as mentioned earlier, longing to break the shackles. The shackles, like most psychological shackles, were "mind-forged manacles," as Blake suggested, and the forge had a complex artistry that displayed its symptoms but not the mold, which remained well hidden. Mr. Perdu was aware that the dream within a dream had exposed the mold more than ever and that the revelation should be pounced on and exploited. "There's loss in one piece of the dream and telling about it in the other," he exclaimed. This eureka of insight provoked a reexamination of all the previously stoked genetic embers. The concepts of "loss" and "telling," themes that were sounded often, were about to lend themselves to variations that surprised the analysand with their novelty, despite their ancient origins. Loss had been a theme that both antedated and postdated the actual childhood loss that occurred, when his older playmates abandoned him. The oedipal years were characterized by incestuous closeness to a mother who had distanced herself from a negligent husband, "seducing" her son, figuratively speaking, with confidences and intimacies that belonged more appropriately in the relationship with her husband.

"There's no telling what I was told," the analysand would quip ironically and cynically as he tried to invoke the childhood atmosphere of loneliness and closeness, a paradox that made more and more sense to him as he explored the absence of his father from his life and the undifferentiated presence of his mother. The "loss" of his father had been passively experienced in the sense that Mr. Perdu never questioned his father's self-destructive character or his mother's compliance with it. He never "told" his father off for his chronic neglect, and he never told his mother off for her abandonment of her dialogue with his father and "seduction" of her son. Instead, he assumed that his loss was coming to him, something he deserved for secretly hating both of them. The actual incident of loss at age five, traumatic and real in itself, was also a screen for deeper losses. Religion was "telling" in the ironic sense that the analysand felt he was telling very private intimacies to the wrong people, priests who in hindsight often seemed unworthy of his revelations. Minor childhood symptoms of latency stealing were adjudicated as major crimes in the confession box, a kind of childhood supreme court that would eventually, of course, take up permanent residence in his superego, through processes of introjection and identification. In retrospect, he realized he hated his mother for supporting a primitive institution that exploited a child's guilt rather than explaining it and exploring it empathically, as analysis would do many years later. "I should have told the priest off. Instead, I swallowed my guts and became a priest myself—identification with the aggressor and victim all at once I suppose." The bitterness of this reconstruction was palpable as insight savored anew the old love, the old hatred, and the relentless conflict.

That his life was about being lost and telling people about it had become more central in the analysis than ever before, thanks to the double vision of the dream and the insight it afforded about the meaning of loss and the meaning of communication (telling) and how both could be corrupted by a defensive psychology that would attempt to keep them apart. "It will be important for me to tell you how much I hate you as termination reprises this sense of loss for yet another time," the analysand said, stepping into the reality of the analytic journey's end with very genuine affect.

The many meanings of the dream-within-dream psychology were uncovered in this rich free-associative process. Telling intimacies to parent, priest, analyst seemed to be one psychological seed of the dream process: loss as experience, loss as unconscious punishment or fear, the other.

The dream thoughts beneath the manifest content of both segments of the dream sequence could be summarized as follows:

The child "delivered" to the house at an "odd" hour is the wish to have a child in the primal scene. The primal crime of the first part of the dream is punished by loss of bearings, loss of home. This stirs up the reality of the actual traumatic loss in childhood, which is reversed in the representation of "a child guided me home." This reversal seems not adequate to the task; "reel switching" becomes necessary. In the "new" dream portion, after the illusion of awakening, there is confession to a bearded man who represents father and analyst (neither one bearded in reality). "Beard" represents undoing of the wish to castrate father and analyst for "forcing" him to confess, for not having a baby with him, for not allowing him to be a permanent analytic baby, for forcing him out as termination approaches. The distance between Connecticut ("connect" as opposite to the "disconnection" of loss) and Greenwich Village is "destroyed," time space altered magically in the new "Greenwich Mean Time" of unconscious timelessness.

This summary does not address the central question I am pursuing even though it is an essential preamble. The analysand's intellectual doggedness about the dream-within-a-dream mechanism was the engine that generated more and more free-associative information about what he playfully referred to as this "unconscious curiosity." The possibility of reaching a compromise between the wish to tell the dream to someone and the wish to stay asleep was entertained as one potential motivation, but there were deeper currents also, he felt sure.

Mr. Perdu was puzzled that the reality of being lost as a child, which had received much scrutiny in the analysis, could still show up in a dream within a dream, as if to insist that it still needed to be disavowed intensely. We had reconstructed pretty well. Which stone had been left unturned? As Mr. Perdu pursued this issue associatively, overwhelming "new" affects appeared genetically and transferentially. Deep-seated anger toward his mother emerged. How could she have entrusted a five-year-old to careless older boys? What did that reveal about the whole ramshackle structure of early care he must have received from a harried young mother starting her own business on the ruins of her husband's psychological and fiscal collapse? Who was this makeshift father? What made him tick? This genetic current of intense affect could turn transferential from hour to hour. What kind of an analyst could have reconstructed so intellectually, leaving the deepest affects untouched? Was the analyst lost in some dream within a dream of his own to have overlooked the most significant meanings? This analytic volatility, genetic and transferential all at once, led to the revelation that the reality of childhood loss had not been fully analyzed, if it ever could be. It was clear that affect would always remain. Sorrow, pain, anger, memory could be understood in analysis but not eliminated, not exorcised. The confessional offered absolution, the wipeout of sin. The couch could offer only understanding, the sober dignity of truth rather than the appeal of illusion!

Communication itself was corrupted in childhood, he believed, when "telling" to a priest became mandatory. Even when he was no longer a priest, the inquisitional dialogue continued within, in the internal confessional. Much of the analytic work in the transference neurosis was an attempt to rehabilitate communication itself, to rescue it from its inquisitional origins. By putting trauma in one dream and "telling" in a dream within it, the analysand was declaring that "telling" was as great a trauma as trauma itself and that the two should not be confused. If he had been able to "tell" his mother off for entrusting him carelessly to the older boys, the original trauma might not have retained its "actual" significance or its symbolic significance as a screen for all the other "tellings" that had been left unsaid. Considering the first part of the dream as the dream within the larger dream (the dream in its totality), the analysand argued that the child guiding him home could be viewed as a fulfillment of the wish that the older boy had not betrayed him or, better still, that he had been able to tell the boy off and demand that the boy not betray him but guide him home. The capacity to talk straight to one's peers in childhood (or adulthood, for that matter) is a measure of how "straight" one felt one could be in the dialogue with father or mother. Developmental achievement cannot be sustained without some early object constancy. If the breast is the first curriculum, baby talk is the first dialogue that leads eventually, developmentally to all later dialogues. Essentially "telling" and "loving" go hand in hand unless the system breaks down for defensive reasons.

If one undoes the division between the two dream parts and treats the text as a seamless document, one reading of the text could be articulated as follows: I want a baby delivered to me in darkness, a primal scene reversal in which I am not excluded. For this the punishment is loss of the object or loss of the love of the object" (castration fear disavowed perhaps as "regressive" object loss screens the more oedipal punishment). "A child guided me home" redresses this. Finally, the wish to tell all to a bearded man represents the undoing of the father's castration and a man-to-man dialogue between son and parent in which aggression and sexuality need not be denied in the new space analysis has cleared for straight talk.

If that was the seamless vision of the dream, why was the illusion of dream within dream necessary at all? To all the defensive reasons alluded to earlier, the analysand added that a dream within a dream is like one dream spawning another. The wish to have the oedipal baby with the analyst, with the mother, with the father, could be represented through the formal disguise of one dream giving birth to another, one dream invaginated in the other in an act of oneiric copulation. One dream was the dream child of the other, so to speak. When the analysis ended, the patient remarked with characteristic irony, "There's no telling what the future holds." While this was obviously true, it seemed clear that the future would hold a more enlightened vision of the past and that a dream within a dream could claim some of the credit for it.

4

CLARENCE'S DREAM IN *RICHARD III*: A DREAM WITHIN A DREAM?

Shakespeare has planted dreams in many of his plays to sharpen the psychological features of a character or to promote dramatic irony. They are all quite effective, but Clarence's dream in act 1, scene 4 of *Richard III* is perhaps his most extraordinary oneiric creation. I believe it may qualify as a dream within a dream, an argument I would like to propose in this brief communication. Harold Bloom (2000) calls Clarence's dream "Shakespeare's dream" to bring emphasis to the stunning artistry of the creator and not just the character. I will present the dream in its entirety; I will define the dynamic structure of dreams within dreams; I then hope to make a convincing case that Clarence's dream is indeed an example of a dream within a dream.

It is a dream related in two parts. Clarence has been confined to the Tower of London, the victim of a piece of treachery engineered by his brother Gloucester—subsequently Richard III—designed to get Clarence, along with many other contenders, "out of his light" so that Gloucester can claim the throne for himself. Clarence is telling his dream to the jail keeper of the Tower, who comments fearfully at times as the nightmarish dream unfolds in Clarence's dramatic retelling of it.

The plot is well known, but I will summarize briefly to give the context out of which the dream emerges. The play begins with Gloucester's famous soliloquy, in which he suggests that since he entered the world "rudely got up" with a deformed body and hunchback, this prenatal, genetic assault on his anatomy entitles him to seek revenge on a world that treats him cruelly. He goes on to describe how he has betrayed his brother Clarence by suggesting to the king that Clarence is plotting against him. King Edward— the brother of Clarence and Gloucester—immediately orders Clarence to be incarcerated in the Tower. Gloucester tells Clarence that he will help to set this straight when in fact he is plotting to send murderers to the Tower to kill Clarence, which does transpire toward the end of act 1, scene 4. The rest of the plot need not concern us except to note that Gloucester does indeed dispatch all rivals to the throne and eventually is crowned Richard III, only to be killed by Richmond in act 5 after a brief reign.

I will focus not only on Clarence's telling of the dream to the jail keeper, but I will also suggest that what happens subsequently in the rest of act 1, scene 4 can be considered Shakespeare's introduction of "associations" into the adjoining text that can be considered as references and afterthoughts to the manifest and latent content of the dream. Here then is the dream in its entirety as Clarence announces it to the jail keeper.

Methoughts that I had broken from the Tower
And was embark'd to cross to Burgundy,
And, in my company, my brother Gloucester,
Who from my cabin tempted me to walk
Upon the hatches. Thence we look'd toward England,
And cited up a thousand heavy times,
During the wars of York and Lancaster,
That had befall'n us. As we pac'd along
Upon the giddy footing of the hatches,

Methought that Gloucester stumbled, and, in falling,
Struck me (that thought to stay him) overboard
Into the tumbling billows of the main.
O Lord, methought what pain it was to drown!
What dreadful noise of waters in my ears!
What sights of ugly deaths within my eyes!
Methought I saw a thousand fearful wracks;
A thousand men that fishes gnaw'd upon;
Wedges of gold, great anchors, heaps of pearl,
Inestimable stones, unvalued jewels,
All scatt'red in the bottom of the sea:
Some lay in dead men's skulls, and in the holes
Where eyes did once inhabit, there were crept
(As 'twere in scorn of eyes) reflecting gems,
That woo'd the slimy bottom of the deep,
And mock'd the dead bones that lay scatter'd by.

The keeper asks in amazement:

Had you such leisure in the time of death
To gaze upon these secrets of the deep?

Clarence answers the keeper's question and then continues to relate his
dream:

Methought I had, and often did I strive
To yield the ghost; but still the envious flood
Stopp'd in my soul, and would not let it forth
To find the empty, vast, and wandering air,
But smother'd it within my panting bulk,

Who almost burst to belch it in the sea.

The keeper, amazed that Clarence didn't wake up at this point, asks:

Awak'd you not in this sore agony?

Clarence answers:

No, no, my dream was lengthen'd after life.
O! then began the tempest in my soul!
I pass'd (methought) the melancholy flood,
With that sour ferryman which poets write of,
Unto the kingdom of perpetual night.
The first that there did greet my stranger soul
Was my great father-in-law, renowned Warwick,
Who cried aloud, "What scourge for perjury
Can this dark monarchy afford false Clarence?"
And so he vanish'd. Then came wand'ring by
A shadow like an angel, with bright hair
Dabbled in blood, and he shriek'd out aloud,
"Clarence is come—false, fleeting, perjur'd Clarence,
That stabb'd me in the field by Tewkesbury:
Seize on him! Furies, take him unto torment!"
With that (methoughts) a legion of foul fiends
Environ'd me, and howled in mine ears
Such hideous cries that with the very noise
I, trembling, wak'd, and for a season after
Could not believe but that I was in hell,
Such terrible impression made my dream.

Let us review the manifest content of this extraordinary dream before we try to fathom the latent content and then ponder whether this dream does indeed harbor the structure of a dream within a dream in its formal design. As pure narrative, the dream has its own excitement, which is enlivened, of course, and made even more dramatic by the interjections of the jail keeper as his anxieties get stirred up by the garish images of Clarence's account. Let us review: Clarence dreams he has escaped from the Tower and in the company of his brother Gloucester has embarked to Burgundy. Gloucester tempts Clarence to walk "upon the giddy footing of the hatches," but when Gloucester stumbles and Clarence tries to stay his fall, Clarence himself is tossed overboard. The latent content cries out for commentary at this point. Clarence's wish to escape from the Tower and expose his brother's treachery (which on some subliminal level he must have sensed) is hidden with great subtlety: "Methoughts" repeated several times in the dream suggests that Clarence knows, at least on an unconscious level, that the reversals he's created in dream content are indeed designed to hide from him his wish to throw his treacherous brother overboard rather than vice versa. Clarence then begins to drown in the sea but not before he describes the visions he saw of shipwrecks, men being gnawed by fish, scattered pearls and gems, some lodged in the eye sockets of skulls, making a mockery of human sight "as 'twere in scorn of eyes." At this point the keeper asks Clarence: "Had you such leisure in the time of death/To gaze upon these secrets of the deep?" Clarence (with yet another "methought") declares that he thought he had "such leisure in the time of death" but then goes on to describe how he struggled to die—"to yield the ghost"—but that the force of the ocean stopped his life in his soul and wouldn't let him belch it out into the "empty vast and wandering air." The jail keeper is astonished at the idea that Clarence could maintain his sleeping state in such nightmarish circumstances and asks: "Awaked you not in this sore agony?" to which

Clarence replies: "No, no, my dream was lengthened after life," and goes on to describe the second portion of his bipartite dream.

In the first segment of this bipartite dream, it is Clarence's denial of what he knows that makes the irony so tragically dramatic. Clarence, hoping to stay the fall of the stumbling Gloucester, is tossed overboard into the raging brine himself. But that is manifest content. Surely the latent unconscious content, which is not characterized by so much denial and disavowal, must deal with a more murderous version of Clarence in which he seeks to toss the stumbling Gloucester overboard. Clarence, after all, in the preceding plays of the tetralogy (*King Henry VI* parts 1, 2, 3, followed by *Richard III*) was a killer himself who dispatched all in his way, not unlike his brother, Gloucester. Perhaps it is Clarence's own guilt, now represented in the second segment of the bipartite dream in the imagery of Warwick and Prince Edward (the "shadow like an angel with bright hair dabbled in blood") accusing him that makes him so gullible to Gloucester's cunning deceits. It is as if the trap that Gloucester set for him had already been self-built in the punitive atmosphere of his own unconscious mind. Rather than throwing Gloucester overboard, he drowns himself in his own suicidal dream. I believe that if Clarence, in analysis, had brought such a dream to the couch, the self-destructive disavowal of mortal danger would certainly have been investigated thoroughly. Manifest defensive disguise would be tracked vigorously to the much blunter truth of the latent dream thoughts.

When Clarence says, "My dream was lengthened after life," does he mean he died in the first part of the dream and then the dream was lengthened into the second equally long portion? Certainly there seem to be two portions of this long dream: had Clarence said not that his dream was lengthened after life but "my dream was lengthened after I thought I had awakened," it would certainly qualify as a dream within a dream. In any case, the two portions seem quite different in tone and content. If the first part deals with Clarence's disavowal of his brother's murderous intent—a disavowal that will not yield to the testimony of reality even as the murderers sent by Gloucester are about to kill him—the second part deals with Clarence's guilt transformed into his own self-appointed Furies that have come to torment him. The two portions of the dream deal with unconscious aggression and unconscious guilt in quite different manners. In the first portion, Clarence seems in awe of the depths he has descended into, a Dante not only terrified but fascinated also by the Inferno he investigates. Guilt has been transformed into a kind of sublimated but exquisite torture. This parade of gnawing images and disemboweled skulls and bones reveals Clarence's aggression almost totally metamorphosed into the sea change of defense so that Clarence seems blissfully unaware of his former murderous nature. Clarence's guilt is much more explicitly imagined in the second portion of the lengthy dream.

If there is a hinge moment connecting the two segments of the dream together in what I would suggest is a *decision* on the dream-work's part to deploy a "dream within a dream" strategy, the statement "No. My dream was lengthened after life" represents that moment. "Dreams within Dreams" (Mahon, 2002) is about the phenomenon of dreams within dreams, suggesting that the two intertwined oneiric envelopes bear an important dynamic relationship with each other. Freud emphasized that whatever content was consigned to the dream within the dream was undoubtedly a reality that was being disavowed by virtue of its banishment out of one dream portion into another. Freud suggested that the comment "it's only a dream" was easy to identify as a wish to obliterate the psychological significance of the whole dynamic nocturnal experience by ridiculing its claims as "such stuff as dreams are mode on." It's only a dream within a dream" would then be a kind of double obliteration of any psychological reality the dream and its meanings might propose or lay claims to. Whereas Freud emphasizes the function of the dream *within* the other dream, Mahon emphasized the dynamic contiguity between the *two* portions, each a dream statement in its own right. Mahon argued that if the first dream's defensive architecture begins to crumble toward nightmare, the second dream may be invoked as a different kind of dynamic tack altogether in the service of disguise and maintenance of the sleeping state. Applying that logic to Clarence's lengthy dream, the dynamic tension between the two portions is highly enlightening. Clarence's dream was about to become alarming to the dream censors (as the frightened jail keeper suggests) so much so that the dream might need to be scuttled altogether by the dream-work as the internal alarms screamed out their anxiety and unhappiness with its failing or already failed sublimations. What to do? The dream-work's job description is to disguise latent intent and content so well that the censor is bemused and sees no cause for censure or alarm. If the blatant aggression of the first portion of Clarence's dream with all its images of death and fishes gnawing on the dead cannot be completely disguised by the strange beauties conjured up by heaps of gold and pearls adorning the eye sockets of the dead, the dream-work, like a juggler with too many balls in the air, decides to ditch all those balls and try a new tactic altogether. Enter the second portion of Clarence's dream, with its new setting and new cast of characters. What I am suggesting is that after Clarence's dream begins so wishfully with the escape from the Tower, the fulfilled wish then seemed to need to be sabotaged by his brother's stumbling and knocking Clarence overboard. But why the need for such self-destruction? The prior tetralogy makes it clear that Clarence is a killer almost the equal of Gloucester in savagery. He can escape from the tower of guilt momentarily but then seems to need to reenter by another unconscious door and imprison himself all over again. Shakespeare seems keenly aware of the workings of such "mind-forged manacles" (Blake, 1795). In that sense the second portion of Clarence's dream is a convoluted example of the dream-work's ingenuities when threatened with collapse of the whole defensive system. If, as already stated, the first portion becomes a catalog of deep-sea horrors as Clarence's aggression masquerades as devouring fishes and human bodies stripped down to bone and pearl-jammed eye sockets, and a death wish thwarted by its inability "to yield the ghost," the second portion suggests that the dream "lengthening" Clarence refers to was a last-minute effort on the part of the dream-work to save the dream from a nightmarish reawakening. To accomplish this, Clarence's dream becomes a sadistic indictment of the self in which Warwick and Prince Edward (the shadow like an angel with bright hair dabbled in blood), having accused him of perjury, set the Furies on him—"a legion of foul fiends"—whose howling eventually awakens the terrified dreamer and keeps him living with the awakened illusion of being in hell "for a season": "such terrible impression made my dream on me."

One last word about the dream lengthening. In the second part of the tetralogy (*King Henry VI*, part 2, act 1, scene2) Shakespeare uses the word "lengthen" in a totally different, but analogous, context. Duchess Eleanor eggs her husband, Duke Humphrey, on to be more ambitious about seeking King Henry's crown for himself. She sees him with his downcast eyes on the ground and teases him about his seeing the crown "in the sullen earth" and that he should reach down and encircle his head with the glorious gold of King Henry's diadem. "Put forth thy hand. Reach for the glorious gold. Was it too short/ I'll lengthen it with mine." In one instance greed is the instigator of lengthening ambition's reach; in the other it is dream illusion that attempts to lengthen the duration of esthetic defense. But is Shakespeare not suggesting something entirely more subtle, more ambitious by this allusion to the same word in decidedly different contexts? Is Shakespeare not suggesting that Clarence's use of the word "lengthen" in relation to the creation of the dream within a dream conceals and reveals all at once a most aggressive, murderous continuation of the concealed aggression in the first dream, just as acquisitive and ambitious as Duchess Eleanor's in *King Henry VI*, part 2? The murderous aggression, which is transformed defensively into its opposite in dream one, will now be changed utterly again in a new fresh defensive posture that calls on the Furies to do its bidding rather than guilty Clarence's recognition and acceptance of his own murderous nature. In other words, Shakespeare's use of "lengthen" in Clarence's words "My dream was lengthened after life" suggests that Clarence, by lengthening his dream after life, still harbors the wish to usurp the crown from his sibling (Edward) as much as Gloucester does even if Clarence needs to disavow it in dream time, a disavowal that eventually leads to his undoing.

I would like to suggest that Shakespeare has indeed given us manifest and latent content of Clarence's dream in act 1, scene 4. If we consider the remaining lines of act 1, scene 4 as associations to this remarkable dream, the arrival of the two murderers and their conflict about whether to kill Clarence or not can be considered as an extension of Clarence's own conscience as it deals with the psychological anguish of his life as slaughterer and now victim of a sibling hatred that is about to be enacted.

When the two murderers arrive, Clarence is sleeping: the murderers deem it unworthy to kill a man who is sleeping since it might be considered cowardly. They have no names: they are referred to as Murderer 1 and Murderer 2. I would like to suggest that the unconscious structure that transforms guilt into self-hatred seems almost nameless and abstract as it delivers its verdict against its victim, the self, guilty as charged. By stripping a portion of the mind of its own identity, hellish indictments can be leveled against the self, as if the self refuses to consider itself human anymore. And yet there is conflict as Murderer 1 and Murderer 2 debate whether they should follow through with Gloucester's wish to clear a pathway to the throne for himself alone by removing all those in his way, including his own brother. The murderers description of conscience and how it gets in the way of decisive action is chilling to the point of being comic. Here is how Murderer 2 describes the tyranny of conscience:

I'll not meddle with it; it makes a man a coward. A man cannot steal, but it accuseth him; a man cannot swear, but it checks him; a man cannot lie with his neighbor's wife, but it detects him. 'Tis a blushing shame-fac'd spirit, that mutinies in a man's bosom. It fills a man full of obstacles. It made me once restore a purse of gold that (by chance) I found. It beggars any man that keeps it. It is turn'd out of towns and cities for a dangerous thing, and every man that means to live well endeavors to trust to himself and live without it.

When Clarence awakens, the three men argue as Clarence pleads and they taunt him with the wrongs he's done. They remind him of his traitorous acts and how his "treacherous blade Unripp'dst the bowels of thy sovereign's son." For all Clarence's pleading, Murderer 1 kills him and throws his body into the Malmsey-butt (a barrel of Malvasian wine), but Murderer 2, invoking Pilate's wish to wash his hands clean of the deadly event, runs off, saying he does not want to be paid by Gloucester after all since he now repents himself.

It is a masterful tragicomic depiction of conscience in general arguing with itself, but if the two murderers are seen as extensions of Clarence's own tormented psyche, it can be viewed as the private hell Clarence finds himself in as he reviews his life of treachery and murder. This depiction of Clarence's guilt and his tormented conflicted management of it is far more psychologically convincing than Gloucester's out-of-character and quite sudden assumption of a mature conscience in act 5 of *Richard III*, which up to that point in the play was decidedly absent. It is as if Shakespeare, at this stage of his development as a playwright, was not yet fully equipped to construct psychologically convincing characters such as Richard II, Hamlet, or Macbeth, and yet in his depiction of Clarence's conflicts and extraordinary dream, he shows he is capable of it once he rids himself of an anxiety of influence (Bloom) that seeks to out-Marlowe Marlowe.

91

By way of concluding remarks, I would like to emphasize that by constructing a dream within a dream, Shakespeare has given extraordinary psychological depth to one character, even if the other depictions of character in the play are shallower. A dream within a dream, by definition, describes a mind that has constructed a dream that fails to contain all the combustible instinctual elements housed within the envelope of itself, and, as a last-ditch effort, extends the envelope that is about to burst its confines in a nightmarish reawakening, thereby creating another dream that gives the illusion that a new dream extension is contained within the other. Whereas Clarence's dream's latent content cries out with murderous sibling rage against his two brothers, Gloucester and Edward (King Edward IV), the manifest content of the hybrid dreams bends over backward unconsciously and defensively to deny, to reverse, to disavow, to project, to turn suicidally against the self, to displace the murderous thrust of all instinctual rage so that Gloucester's treachery is denied right up to the moment of Clarence's immersion in the Malmsey-butt! In the first portion of the double-barreled dream, Clarence's desire to throw Gloucester overboard gets reversed so that its murderous intent can be turned into a death wish against the self. When the self-preserving self is unable to belch itself into the sea, a second dream is called upon, in which Clarence goes to hell to see the sour ferryman and have the Furies turned against him by those victims he has dispatched in the past. The aggression in the first portion of the dream tries suicide as a desperate but unsuccessful solution to contain itself, but that comes close to scuttling the whole dream's defensive architecture until dream portion number two tries an alternate tactic. A menacing, hellish superego (the Furies) summoned from the afterlife tries to disguise all the instinctual fury in an assault of barbarous conscience, and when that fails, Clarence wakes up in a nightmare that seems to last "a season" so real did the dream affects seem to the dreamer. By constructing such a dream and assigning it to a relatively minor character in a five-act play, Shakespeare has plumbed the depths of dream life a few hundred years before Freud even introduced the concept of dreams within dreams. Was Shakespeare a Freudian? Bloom has suggested that such a question is better answered with another question: Was Freud a Shakespearean? Surely the answer to both questions is a resounding yes.

THE UNCANNY IN A DREAM

5

In this chapter I focus on an instance of the uncanny in a dream and speculate on the particular function such an inclusion might have served. A patient dreamed about the proper name of an author (Thomas B. Costain), which he believed at first to be a fictitious dream concoction. In fact, all his initial associations dealt with the dream inclusion as if it had no connection to reality. When he later googled the name "for the hell of it," he was surprised to uncannily discover that what he was referring to as "that strange dream name" was in fact the proper name of a moderately well-known twentieth-century author! His subsequent discovery that one of the author's books, *The Silver Chalice*, reminded him of silver paper chalices his father used to make for him as a child jolted him further. This revived repression, not only of an author's name, but of its significant connection to repressed genetic memories, filled him with a sense of awe, as if he had suddenly been awakened from a hypnotic spell. If dream experience in general can be considered uncanny, I argue that the dream-work deployed this *particular* inclusion of an uncanny "fictitious" representation of reality for complex dynamic reasons.

The whole dreaming process could be considered uncanny, of course, but I want to draw attention to a particular isolated instance within the total fabric of a single dream. Having associated to all the elements in the dream, including what he believed to be the fictitious name (Thomas B. Costain), he googled the name, expecting to find that the fictitious name was indeed a concoction of the dream-work. He was amazed to discover that the "fictitious" name did, in fact, correspond to the letter, even the middle initial, to the real name of a rather famous author! Thomas B. Costain, born in Canada in 1885, was at first a journalist, but he began to write historical novels in his fifties, one of them—*The Silver Chalice*—a bestseller that spawned a famous movie starring Paul Newman. *The Silver Chalice* refers to a fictional chalice that was made to house the wooden goblet Christ used at the Last Supper. What was truly uncanny for the analysand was that as a child his father used to make him silver chalices out of the silver paper his cigarettes came wrapped in. The uncanny, in this particular instance, seemed to have retrieved at least two significant repressed components from the past: silver chalices offered as playthings by the father and a fictitious name that turned out to be real. There was a transference context, of course: all sorts of artifacts from the past had already appeared over a lengthy process of excavation. Initially, the analyst believed the name Thomas B. Costain also to be a concoction of the dream-work. The analyst's ignorance could be attributed to the fact that he had arrived as a young physician in New York in the sixties, and many aspects of the culture had not been incorporated by him. He had never heard of Costain or the Paul Newman movie *The Silver Chalice*. The analysand's initial ignorance did seem, however, to be a dynamic issue of great significance.

The dream should be presented at this point so that the reader can appreciate the uncanny in statu nascendi just as the dreamer did.

I am at a conference. A journalist is being interviewed. His name is Thomas. B. Costain. The interviewer inappropriately asks the journalist if his chronic depression had compromised his professional life in any way. I cringe at the interviewer's crassness and would have undone the insult if I could.

Before I present the collaborative analytic work on this dream, a few words about the uncanny, in general, are in order. Freud's paper "The Uncanny" was published in 1919. He refers to "this modest contribution of mine" as having been affected by "the times in which we live," a reference to the war Europe and the rest of the world was trying to recover from. In his paper Freud concluded that uncanny experiences occur "when infantile complexes which have been repressed are once more revived by some impression, or when primitive beliefs which have been surmounted seem once more to be confirmed." Freud, like most of the intellectuals of the time, believed that the First World War would restructure the world in some romantic idealistic manner. Looking back with hindsight on the folly of such romantic idealism, one can only assume that some uncanny "infantile complexes" or primitive unsurmounted beliefs had indeed usurped the common sense of a whole generation of thinkers.

Freud was fascinated with the antithetical meaning of primal words in general and with the etymology of the word "uncanny" (*"unheimlich"* in German) in particular. In German, the *"heimlich"* and the *"unheimlich"* can be equally disquieting in connotation. The same is true for "canny" and "uncanny" in English. Freud suggests that when the "familiar" (infantile complexes) is repressed and then revived by "some impression," an uncanny affect occurs. Since it is the "familiar" parent that the child wants to engage in incest or murder, no wonder the child invokes amnesia as the ultimate resolution. But amnesia is always relative: "some impression" can, when least expected, trigger a return of the repressed. Having very briefly reprised Freud's ideas on the uncanny, I will now return to the discussion of the dream and describe the impression in consciousness (the days' residue) that got the whole manifest and latent choreography started.

The analysand, intrigued with the mise-en-scène of the dream, began to free associate immediately to the fictional name, as if it were a fabrication of days' residues and ancient artifacts. On a recent short trip to Italy, he had heard a politician named Costa pitching his case for election to an audience in the town square. He had been at a mercatino (a small Italian outdoor market) earlier that day, and one of the vendors was inviting people to sample his wares, proclaiming: "Cedere, cedere, costa niente," which means "yield, yield, my products cost nothing." Associating to "cost" in "costain," the analysand became aware that the cost of analysis seemed to be on his mind. He was convinced that the issue of a product that cost nothing had insinuated itself into the dream. (It seemed clear that "cost" and "costa" were the impressions in consciousness that had awakened disturbing, unconscious affects.) "I wish analysis cost nothing" was the obvious implication, and that analytic love was unconditional as opposed to market driven. Continuing to take each phoneme of the dream apart, he associated to the "stain" in Costain. "We are all stained with mortality," he reflected, his anger at the analyst's "conditional" love deflected onto a more defensive, philosophical plane. He associated to "Thomas" as the name of his dead brother and to the middle initial *B* as "to be or not to be" from Hamlet's soliloquy. He associated the whole name "Thomas B. Costain" as not too dissimilar from the analyst's, which also had the middle initial *J*. When the transference was at its most ambivalent, the analysand had often joked that *J* stood for Jesus or Judas, a piece of irony I will return to later.

Up to this point the analysand had been free associating to Thomas B. Costain as a fictitious name, a proper name concocted solely by the dream-work's artistry. It came as a shock to him when he googled and discovered that Thomas B. Costain was, in fact, the name of a real journalist/novelist. This uncanny experience was rendered even more disquieting as he began to reflect on the strange coincidence of his father's gifts of the childhood chalices and the completely repressed name of a novelist who had written a famous book called *The Silver Chalice*. For it was beginning to dawn on him that a significant act of "repression" was the only way to explain the seemingly total ignorance of an author whose name and novels had been stored with such accuracy in the forgotten files of memory. The correct assignation of the dream "Thomas B. Costain" as not only a novelist, but a journalist as well, seemed yet another instance of the uncanny. If the dream in toto was uncanny, these precise particulars seemed to out-uncanny the uncanny.

The eventual interpretation of the dream that emerged from the collaborative analytic process could be summarized as follows: the analysand acknowledged to himself that he is not only the cringing embarrassed observer in the dream but also the brash reporter who embarrasses Thomas B. Costain with the question about his chronic depression. The analysand was able to admit to himself that he would have liked to have had the courage to challenge his father directly rather than transforming his anger always into masochism, guilt, defensive identification, reaction formations. In a sense, the gift of the silver chalices was a screen for all the developmental gifts the father had deprived him of. The father was indeed a writer (not as famous as Thomas B. Costain) and a university lecturer. But he had a chronic manic-depressive illness, which was reflected in frequent unemployment issues. The father had moved his family from city to city many times in pursuit of more and more elusive employment. The analysand could hardly keep track of all the different grade schools he had attended, but he believed it might have been as many as eleven or twelve in five or six years.

The analysand was, of course, intrigued by the uncanny structure of the dream. At first he believed he had never heard of Thomas B. Costain before in his life and that the strange appearance of the name had to be a magical confluence of accidentals, similar to a monkey writing the script of *Hamlet* by chance if the monkey had forever to work on it. But then, as alluded to earlier, a more probable explanation dawned on him: he must at some point in his life have heard of Thomas B. Costain. What's more, he must have known Costain wrote *The Silver Chalice*. He must have repressed the information at a period in his life when the ambivalence about his father (the traumatic neglect as well as the poignant compensatory childhood gifts) was too painful to acknowledge and had to be removed completely from consciousness. Years must have passed before the repressed was able to represent itself again in the free-associative climate of analysis in an uncanny manner in a dream. The initial repression was most impressive: the return of the repressed in the dream brought no affect of recognition in its wake, unless one argues that the decision to google the name Thomas B. Costain had some premonitory trace of recognition in it in the first place.

Some genetic material is essential at this point to illuminate the appearance of the uncanny. The analysand had an older brother Thomas who was cognitively impaired. This brother had died recently, and Thomas B. Costain was in part a reference to this tragedy. Though cognitively impaired his brother was nevertheless an accomplished swimmer. When he died in a freak accident in the ocean, the analysand was plunged into an extraordinary episode of grief that he believed was twofold: it represented grief for the brother, to be sure, but also an unrelenting grief about the loss of his father, not only through death itself but through the even greater loss of life lived to the fullest that chronic depression entails. He became aware that Thomas B. Costain wove together so many overdetermined threads in the fabric of his unconscious. Intense analytic process on these issues unearthed a most significant unconscious fantasy: "My father, my brother, and I are *costained* forever with the undifferentiated magic of genetic life." The middle initial, *B,* refers to "to be or not to be," a declaration of symbiotic suicidal codependence that tries to erase guilt from the wake of robust individuation through regressive nonindividuation. "If only I could be *costained* forever with father and brother, I would never have to recognize

100

my unique differentiation from both of them." (I have summarized months of analytic process in the service of aligning the uncanny nature of the analytic process with the uncanny nature of genetic psychology.)

Let us consider the dream in statu nascendi. The initial dream thoughts ("I hate my father for neglecting me. I'd like to interview him and embarrass him with the truth and expose his irresponsibility for all the world to see") need to be disguised. This direct vehement exposure and critique of the father needs to be sanitized. The dream-work "decides" to displace the direct critique onto the "interviewer," while the personification of the dreamer "cringes" in embarrassment at the interviewer's crassness. If the dream conflict divided up in this manner is not enough of a defensive disguise to keep the manifest level from revealing too much latent content, the dream-work can call up the reserves, so to speak. Enter Thomas B. Costain, a fictitious-sounding name if ever there was one. The supreme irony is, of course, that only the dream-work (assuming that all repressed content is available to it, and it can, like a painter, choose any unconscious pigment it likes to produce its effects) knows at this point that Thomas B. Costain is indeed a real writer! In fact, if the dreamer had by chance been reading about Thoams B. Costain a few days before this particular dream was "assembled" and the repressed had thereby been returned to him, surely the dream-work could not have used reality masquerading as fiction in such a manner. The dream does seem to flirt with exposure by employing Thomas B. Costain as a decoy, not unlike a cheater in a card game revealing a protruding sliver of the hidden ace up his sleeve. All defense seems to ride on such irony as if the wish to reveal and the wish to conceal thrived on such ambivalence (Shafer, 1968). In the case of Thomas B. Costain, the dream-work seems to rely on the solidity and stability of repression as if the awakener's eventual decision to google can be discounted as a most unlikely possibility. In a sense the awakener's reaction is Sophoclean: Oedipus insists on pursuing the truth even when he knows it will spell his own doom. The dramatic irony of Sophocles's play rests after all on the idea that the audience knows everything before Oedipus stumbles on it, just as the dream-work knew what it was concealing from the dreamer before the oracular google spilled the beans and just as the awakener on some level knew what he had repressed so dramatically many years ago. *The Silver Chalice*, Thomas B. Costain, Paul Newman, as well as the much earlier memory of silver paper chalices made by a tragically depressed man who wanted to offer his son more than his constitutional endowment would allow him, all played their part in the construction of the dream. As analytic insights over time allowed the analysand to reflect deeply on the nature of his father's chronic mental illness, the silver paper chalices became a great symbol of love and hate, satisfaction and deprivation, instinct and repression, tragic loss and resilient resignation. "You can't give what you don't have," he would wryly say when sympathy for his father's illness outweighed his resentment. There was bitterness in such wry commentary and sober reflection, too. To become the "new man" analysis projected, his guilt about his death wishes toward his father and brother and "incestuous possession" of his mother would have to be revised and reclaimed from the tragic neurotic conviction that he was as tragically "costained" with depression, death, and failure as his father and brother were. As the analysis nears termination, the analysand has come to realize among other things that though all men are "costained" with mortality, neurotic defensive unanalyzed identifications with the dead—or the living, for that matter— need not "costain" us all in some kind of symbiotic blindness that would make independent individuated ambitious exuberant pre-oedipal and oedipal life impossible.

Freud argued that the uncanny had several components. He made a distinction between the inheritance of those component "animistic" elements that are "surmounted" in the course of civilized development and the repressed components that have more to do with psychodynamic infantile life and its conflicts. When either the "surmounted" or the "repressed" returns, the analysand feels an uncanny affect. Freud agreed that both the surmounted and the repressed could operate in conjunction. The uncanny affect would seem to be that moment of surprise when complacent repression assumes that the objectionable has been censored only to discover that the dream interviewer for instance, like a child in a Hans Christian Andersen story, is bound to confront the emperor's self-deception with its full-frontal nakedness. When the dreamer awakens into the uncanny nakedness of himself, or when the free-associative transferential process awakens into the surprise of its own forgotten genetics, the emperor is willing to relinquish his defensive omnipotence and reclaim the little kingdom of reality where there are no kings at all. At that moment the seemingly fictitious Thomas B. Costain and the very real writer of the same name will recognize each other in the aesthetics of dream analysis as the repressed returns and is no longer afraid of itself.

If dream is a compromise between instinct and repression, a compromise that teasingly manifests a portion of itself while rigorously hiding the most significant aspects of itself, this drama of exhibition and disguise is always on the verge of esthetic exhaustion and collapse. When the esthetic "suspension of disbelief" begins to falter and the dreamer suspects and fears a sudden descent into nightmare or into rude awakening and panic, the dream-work exploits all of its resources to keep more and more balls of disguise in the air. I have argued that when a dream, which is after all a pretty uncanny disguise in toto, highlights one particular instance of the uncanny, the alert dream interpreter will recognize the introduction of the uncanny as a desperate cover-up maneuver designed to disguise a major fault line in the overall structure of the dream. Such an alert dream interpreter will recognize the uncanny red herring and not be fooled by the dream-work's impressive sleight of hand.

6

A FILM IN A DREAM

The manifest content of a dream is cinematic almost by definition: as Freud intuited in his picket fence analogy in chapter seven of *The Interpretation of Dreams*, the conscious world as worded reality becomes the unconscious world as unworded surreality, as words are changed into wordless images. One can already experience this metamorphosis of word into image as one falls asleep as Silberer (1909) showed, in clinical illustrations, now called the Silberer phenomenon after the gifted, if tragic, psychoanalyst. Why then, if the dream is practically a film already, is there a need in certain dreams for the mise-en-scène of the dream to create the illusion that the dream is not a dream but a film? That is the question I would like to focus on in this chapter.

The dreamer is a ninety-year-old man who was analyzed successfully (with a termination worked out in a mutual agreement) thirty years earlier. He is a professor of English literature, a prolific writer, and still intellectually active. His wife died a year ago and he has returned to examine a grief that shows no signs of lessening. He imagines his dead wife still walks around the apartment, even hallucinating her at times. This is very disturbing and debilitating. He knows it is a dramatization of his conflict about letting go and holding on, but this insight does not always bring relief. One major issue in the earlier analysis had been his rage at and disappointment in dysfunctional parents and the rerouting of that rage into self-hatred orchestrated by a primitive superego. The analysis had made it possible for him to claim the anger as the agency of an empowered ego, which in turn modified the hegemony of the primitive superego significantly. There were regressions, of course, when the superego returned to its savage role of guilty self-annihilator. With rigorous self-analysis he could realign the balance of power again, the ego reclaiming its position as executor of a well-integrated mind. But there were human limits, of course. The loss of his wife after sixty-five years of marriage had removed a cornerstone of his life and stability, and he could feel the psychological edifice beginning to crumble. He sensed that regression to primitive self-hating guilty attacks on a grieving self were at the core of his current misery for which he was now seeking what he believed could be a brief bout of analysis to address this.

He always had dreamed copiously and readily, remembering and retaining his dreams in an impressive manner. His older sister lives in London. Both were born in London, but the older sister has lived there all her life (let us call her Mary), while the dreamer (let us call him Peter) left London in his twenties for New York to advance his career. He had been offered a professorship at a major institution, an opportunity he could not turn down. He has lived in New York ever since, making frequent trips to London and the Continent every year. With this minimal sketch of his life to orient us, let us examine the dream in question closely.

The Dream

The dream feels like a film from start to finish. That is the sensation throughout the whole dream mise-en-scène. The opening shots show the London sky with the tall buildings piercing the skyscape. The buildings are all covered with striped carpet. The stripes are perpendicular and are ochred with earth colors. The buildings are left partially uncarpeted in places so that you can see the effect. Gene

106

Wilder and another actor are in a museum but hurrying to make sure they can get to the theater before the end of the performance. Gene Wilder is carrying a carpet. He carries it past a painting in the museum. The woman depicted in the painting vanishes from the canvas as Gene Wilder passes by. You realize that the woman is now secreted in the carpet as if this were a planned heist. The men go out on the street. It's Leicester Square. A woman is pointing at several passersby. She alludes to the many Lesters who have died, Leicester Square accentuating this in some macabre fashion.

Peter associates to all the images in the dream. Lester Young, the great jazz saxophonist, who accompanied Billie Holiday has a reference to "young" in his surname, youth being a most wishful fantasy of Peter's as he and his sister age and get closer to the edge of mortality. His sister is five years older, and he fears he will never see her alive again if the COVID pandemic keeps making it too dangerous for him to fly. He feels so guilty about canceling a recent trip to London. He believes that the *car* in "carpet" is a wish that the Atlantic did not separate London from New York and that he could drive safely to London. He continues to associate to carpet, which has *carpe* in it, as in "carpe diem." "Not so many more days left to carpe," he says bitterly. Why are the buildings in London carpeted? Is it a wish to keep London swathed in carpet and protect it from the bombs of childhood? He is referring to the Blitz in London in 1941. He was about nine years old, his sister fifteen. His dysfunctional parents calmed their anxieties with alcohol, but Mary, a remarkably self-possessed young woman, calmed the nine-year-old Peter by her confident presence and emotional aplomb. Peter would never forget it. Angry as he was at his parents, who were brilliant intellectuals but knew practically nothing about parenting, his vision of Mary as the epitome of courage was as close to the experience of a functioning parent as he ever experienced. He remembers her putting a moist handkerchief on his forehead when he was afraid in the subways as the bombs whistled, and the feel of moist cloth had an enormous therapeutic effect on him. The experience is one that he can call up to soothe himself whenever he feels overwhelmed psychologically.

Leicester Square brought associations about the First World War song "It's a long way to Tipperary," whose lyrics refer to Leicester Square (*Goodbye Picadilly, Farewell Leicester Square*). It was a song written in 1912 and sung by soldiers leaving home and worrying about never seeing Leicester Square again. Peter was also afraid of never seeing Leicester Square again, or his sister alive again, for that matter.

Gene Wilder and his colleague hurrying so as not to miss the end of the theatrical performance refers to Peter's wish to see his sister before the final curtain.

Gene Wilder spiriting the woman from painting to carpet seemed like a wish to rescue his sister from her fate. He imagined the painting being Wyeth's *Christina's World*, a depiction of a woman with a degenerative disease who hated to use a wheelchair, preferring to crawl along the fields that surrounded her house. Peter felt that this association was an obvious reference to his wish to save his sister from death and carry her away in a magic carpet to immortality. He knew that it could also be a reference to his recently deceased wife, whom he was still hallucinating in his grief.

"What incredible deceptions the dream-work concocts as it distorts everything in its convex mirror," Peter said sadly, displaying the knowledge of psychoanalysis his experience and vast reading had amassed over the years.

Peter continued to have associations to carpet. He had a literary reference to the idea of their being a *carp* in "carpet." He quoted Polonius's speech to Reynaldo in act 2, scene 1 of *Hamlet* in which Polonius is trying to get Reynaldo to get the dirt on his son Laertes while he is away from the court. He advises Reynaldo to spread some lies about Laertes in the hope that as people deny the lies, they may reveal some truths about his son's behavior. "Your bait of falsehood takes this carp of truth." The father is instructing Reynaldo how to get at the truth through falsehood ("by indirections find directions out"). "Not unlike the dream," Peter says with mischievous intent. I believe he meant that if the latent content is the repository of psychoanalytic truth, it must be approached by checking out all the "lies" the manifest content concocts in the service of evading the dream censor and securing a good night's sleep!

Peter had one last association to carpet: there is a *pet* in it, an association that led him back to the Blitz, the moist handkerchief on his forehead as his five years older sister, Mary, petted him out of his fears. She was more parent to him than his actual parents, and not being able to travel to London to see her stirred up a guilt that he knew was one of the factors at the core of his dreams. He wondered if his genes were wilder than hers, as he associated to the presence of Gene Wilder in the dream. She seemed so calm and secure while he was easily moody and agitated. He did not associate to the Gene in the analyst's name, and the analyst decided not to drag the transference in at this venue. Another association to Gene Wider referred to Mel Brooks's film *Young Frankenstein*, a hilarious cinematic farce that Peter was very moved by. The reference to Frankenstein was, of course, in part about resurrecting the dead, a wish at the core of his unconscious that he could not deny as he imagined his dead wife and Mary edging closer to the end of life.

Why film? Peter would ask as he mused about the whole striking *form* of the dream. He had many ideas. A dream is so easily forgotten, whereas film can be preserved and archived, thereby living forever. Talking films were just taking off when his sister was born, and film has become a dominant portion of culture ever since. Film invites fantasies of immortality. On the following evening, Peter had another dream in film format that really intrigued him. He had never dreamed about film before, and now here was another example on the following night.

I will describe the dream before I continue with an attempt to make sense of both dreams.

The Dream

An opening shot of John Wayne beside a huge oak tree begins the sequence. Then a boy appears searching for his lost ball. It has become trapped in the exposed roots of the giant tree. John Wayne releases the ball from its captivity, places it squarely on a leveled area of ground beyond the roots, and kicks it up into the sky. The boy chases after it gleefully and catches it expertly out of the sky like a pro. As he catches the ball, he looks back over his shoulder, grinning gratefully at the larger-than-life place-kicker. A priest on a hill close by starts shooting darts at John Wayne from a contraption that looks like a makeshift propulsion weapon. The darts are propelled by the priest's mouth through the aperture in the weird invention. John Wayne becomes irate and chases after the priest to protest. As John Wayne tries to climb up to where the priest is, the priest tries to block his ascent, but John Wayne succeeds in climbing up and a fight ensues between the two men.

Peter never liked John Wayne's politics—or his acting skills, for that matter—and he became convinced that it must be the spelling of the name that earned John Wayne a place in the manifest dream content. He began to associate to "Wayne," turning it into "wane," as in the waning and waxing of the moon, or the waning of human life as time thoughtlessly proceeds on its quantum path toward infinity. The boy and the ball would elicit the opposite kind of associations, the waxing of young life as opposed to the waning of it. The priest shooting darts at John Wayne made Peter think of all those depictions in art of death personified as a creature visiting its fatal arrows upon those who must die. The boy with the ball looking back gratefully at the larger-than-life film star made Peter associate to his dysfunctional father: in his fantasy, in an alternate version of reality, it is Mary who kicks the ball into the sky and Peter the boy who so expertly retrieves it.

A discussion of all of Peter's many associations to the two dreams must begin with a pedantic distinction. These "films" are, strictly speaking, not *in* the dream but have rather co-opted the whole form of the dream and created the illusion that Peter is not watching a film in a dream but watching a film itself. The question then, of course, becomes, Why did the dream-work, that impresario of illusion, need to create such an illusion in the first place? In other instances of unusual inclusions in dreams, I have argued that the insertion of something novel into a dream—a parapraxis, a pun, a joke, et cetera—is designed to rivet attention on the manifest novelty so that the dreamer or the dream censor is unaware that sexual or murderous instinct has been disguised cleverly to elude the consciousness of dreamer or censor. Following that line of argument, the illusion that the dreamer is watching a movie must be a necessary aspect of disguise in these instances. "It's only a film" must be something equivalent to "It's only a dream" as a statement of innocence as the dream-work plots its campaign of sneaking salacious combustible murderous intent and content past the censor. What then, in Peter's case, is the objectionable material being sneaked past the customs officials of sleep?

One of the great affects that Peter was aware of was his fury, conscious to some extent and repressed to an even greater extent. He sensed that the repressed fury, turned against the self, was creating havoc within, a havoc of depression and self-laceration. The dreams, masquerading as films, were an attempt to put a film over all these issues, a veneer of sublimation. It would be very easy to focus on the entertainment the films provided and

111

lose sight of the latent dream content. But Peter had come to work and get to the bottom of what was becoming a pathological mourning rather than a grief that would release him eventually from its shackles and return him to normal life. He knew that "normal life" might be a long time coming in a world in the grip of a pandemic, but he knew that nonneurotic life even in a pandemic was worth fighting for. And fighting had to begin with finding the latent content and using that material to further his recovery.

There was more than fury, of course, at the root of the dreaming process. There was magical fulfillment of wishes. A woman was being spirited off a painting and hidden in a carpet so that the dreamer could walk out of the museum without being suspected of larceny. A great wish was being expressed to save his wife, save his sister. But even in the dream, when he walks out of the museum, he is confronted by death (the two Lesters who have died). And Leicester Square, that reminder of all the dead lost in the follies of the First World War. Lester Young revealed the wish for youth that could postpone thoughts of death for decades of denial.

A week later Peter had another film dream that was really more nightmare than dream. This dream alarmed him not only because it was yet another film dream but because of its terrifying content.

Again there is the illusion that Peter is watching a film rather than a dream.

A boy in a desert is looking up at a slit in the mountainside, like an observation window. Behind the slit are boys or young men with machine guns. They seem to be contemplating whether to shoot at the boy for sport or not to. The dreamer seems to be aware of this and says to himself, "This movie is predictable. I don't have to watch any more of this." And he decides to walk on, turning away from the mountain and traversing a different terrain. In this new locality, a trial is being conducted. A man is being accused of sexual crimes. The woman may be there also, but it is the man who is being judged. The man has contempt for this mock trial, and he rails against his accusers. It feels like a Taliban court, where the outcome has already been decided. While he rails, his accusers are mocking him and laughing at him. Then you see a man in a white coat, such as a butcher or a surgeon. This man is sweating profusely and shaking with fear. It is clear in this film dream that his job is to carve up the accused man who has been sentenced to death. It is not clear whether he will be carving a dead corpse or carving a living person. The dreamer awakens in horror and turns over in his bed to assure himself that his wife is okay only to discover, of course, that his wife has been dead for the past year.

Peter related this dream with a sense of amazement. It was clear that the shock of it had not quite left him as he spoke. He was surprised that this dream represented another film dream, but it was the manifest dream content that really shocked him. He'd had nightmares before, but this one reminded him of the primal scene content we had worked on intensely in the earlier analysis many years ago. He was referring to a specific memory of a childhood dream: in the dream, he was looking at a frame on the wall of his bedroom. The painting began to develop a diagonal slit that tore across the surface, breaking the frame. Behind the frame the bedroom wall began to crack open, revealing two candles that were flickering, their flames beginning to encroach his bedroom. The child awoke in a panic. This "primal scene" had many layers to it. At the time of the earlier analysis, Peter had related this to his fears about his parents, who, when intoxicated, could fight loudly. It never came to blows, but the sound of two people raising their voices had frightened him way beyond childhood, until he set things straight in a lengthy analysis. His anger at his parents for frightening him could not be addressed until his anger became an emotion he could possess and value as an important portal of communication.

Another layer of this "primal scene" had been minted in the undergrounds during the Blitz. Once, while in the tube taking refuge from an air raid, by candlelight he saw a woman nursing her child. He was surprised by the size of the breast, and he was aware that he was also sexually aroused by it. He also felt guilt that he was looking at all and had to close his eyes and turn away. In the course of his analysis, Peter became aware that his normal childhood feelings of sexual curiosity and anger at parents who neglected him or frightened him had gone underground before they surfaced again in analysis. He thought that the candles that could invade his bedroom represented not only his sexual curiosity—throwing a light on things—but also his burning rage that could inflame his home and burn it down. The Blitz was a terror that colored all of this as well.

The dream about the Taliban and the slit in the mountainside elicited many associations. He had a childhood memory about the "slit" between a girl's thighs—his way of depicting the vagina—and the castration fears that the anatomical sexual distinction aroused in him. In the memory, he has a bruised knee, which is quickly recovering. He remembers wishing it would not recover so fast since he was reluctant to part with all the attention he received while he was in the injured state. He also associated "slit" with the nightmare in which the man in the white coat might have to slit the accused man's throat and then carve up the rest of him. Peter chuckled, saying, "This was a "crimal" scene as well as a primal scene." The humor was dark and still retained a modicum of fear in it.

Peter then turned his attention to the need to wrap the whole nightmarish dream in a celluloid film of illusion. He was baffled. The ability to say "it was only a film" or "it was only a dream" was surely significant, but was there more method in the madness the dream-work

114

had concocted? Etymology suggests that "film" has its roots in Old English "filmen," meaning membrane, thin skin, foreskin. Did this etymological link spill over into the nightmare of the white-coated butcher skinning the man accused of sexual assault alive?

Talking about all these associations gave Peter a sense of control over this X-rated film that had invaded his nightlife. He was deeply shocked, of course, as he stretched his arm out of the nightmare to check on his wife to make sure she was okay only to be startled to discover her absence. He knew that his grief at his wife's absence as well as his frustration that he could not travel to London to see his sister were probably the emotional engine that fired up these dreams of horror and loss. John Wayne ready to fight with death personified as a priest said it all in a way. Peter wanted to put his anger to work and not be bullied by the death instinct—make his anger work for him in a practical manner. He knew that would help him to deal with the reality of his difficult situation, by taking neurotic magical thinking out of the equation. His power should not reside in butchers of conscience that would skin him alive. He needed the full force of his rage to be housed in the agency of his ego, which would allow him to proceed cautiously but surefootedly through a pandemic that had diminished his options but not his resilience. He would fly to London when the all clear was sounded by science and medicine and facts and not by merchants of disinformation. This would not bring endless happiness, but it would allow him to grieve, put the past in its place, and do the best he could with the present. It was okay to put a film over reality temporarily, but eventually the film has to be removed. One must awaken from dreams and put them to work, as Freud has counseled us, the better to chart our course through the waters of reality. Peter had one other association to the four Lesters mentioned in his dreams (two good friends, Lester Young the musician and Leicester Square). "There is a 'lest' in Lester," he said, which brought to mind a Nietzsche quote he would cite for his colleagues. He had cited it often in the prior analysis. "We have art lest we perish from the truth." Peter used to like to turn the phrase around and say, "And we have truth lest we be diverted by art that might try to steer us away from processing reality wisely." You can throw a film over the content of a dream the better to disguise its unconscious message, but it is wise to remove it eventually so that the latent meanings of the dream can enlighten the awakener once he has allowed the work of analysis to retrieve all that the dream-work has so masterfully and so artfully disguised.

7

A PARAPRAXIS IN A DREAM

Now we turn from humor and puns in dreams to study a parapraxis in a dream. When a parapraxis is put on display in a dream, one can only wonder what service the willful mistake is rendering to resourceful dream-work. Freud taught us that anything that appears in the manifest content of a dream may well be a disguise or a distortion of a subject that originally made an anxiety-provoking, and hence short-lived, first appearance in latent dream thoughts. Dreams within dreams and jokes in dreams have been examined from this perspective, and now we focus on the appearance and meaning of a parapraxis in a dream, with the argument that seemingly casual "mistakes" are highlighted in the manifest display to cover up some latent, much more deliberate subject matter.

One of Freud's (1900) comments on parapraxes in dreams is sweepingly reductionistic, yet powerful. In addressing déjà phenomena in dreams, he writes: "In some dreams of landscapes or other localities, emphasis is laid in the dream itself on a convinced feeling of having been there once before. These places are invariably the genitals of the dreamer's mother; there is indeed no other place about which one can assert with such conviction that one has been there once before" I.D. (p. 399).

If Freud's assessment of parapraxes in dreams sounds like a recklessly intuitive generalization about the meaning of déjà vu, in another instance, he follows the clinical material in a less sweeping, more focused manner. He reports one of his own dreams:

> I was going to the hospital with P., through a district in which there were houses and gardens. At the same time I had a notion that I had often seen this district before in dreams. I did not know my way about very well. He showed me a road that led round the corner to a restaurant (indoors, not a garden). There I asked for Frau Doni and was told that she lived at the back in a small room with three children. I went toward it, but before I got there met an indistinct figure with my two little girls; I took them with me after I had stood with them for a little while. Some sort of reproach against my wife, for having left them there.
>
> When I woke up I had a feeling of great satisfaction, the reason for which I explained to myself as being that I was going to discover from this analysis the meaning of "I've dreamed of that before." In fact, however, the analysis taught me nothing of the kind; what it did show me was that the satisfaction belonged to the latent content of the dream and not to any judgment upon it. My satisfaction was with the fact that my marriage had brought me children. P. was a person whose course in life lay for some time alongside mine, who then outdistanced me both socially and materially, but whose marriage was childless [Freud, 1900, p. 446–447)

Freud sweeps the anagogic interpretation of his own dream aside as too facile to engage him beyond the first waking moments and reaches deeper for the psychoanalytic meaning: a wish to topple a rival, on the most sexual turf ("my flesh is procreative, and yours isn't!"). Freud, initially seduced by the manifest satisfaction of discovering the meaning of "I've dreamed that before," is not satisfied (ironically enough) until he traces

118

the sense of satisfaction to its deeper, darker core of meaning in the realm of competitive, sexual latent imagery. But, by focusing on the affect of satisfaction, Freud neglects the formal structure of parapraxis itself and its functional defensive armature, and to this neglected aspect of the topic I would like to bring emphasis. It is Freud's revolutionary insight that allows us to understand that intellectual assessment made in the manifest content of a dream should be seen as a disguised derivative of a latent issue: in other words, it is subordinate to the main agenda of the dream, which is dream-work, even though its manifest content usurps the limelight in its overt display.

Whereas Freud suggests that déjà vu is a reference to the universal spawning ground of the mother's genital, a place about which everyone could assert, "I have been here before," I would like to argue that a parapraxis that claims "to have been here before" is making a rightful claim from another vantage point: since it has been displaced from its original latent context to its more high-profile, manifest role of disguise, it has made a prior appearance in dream space and is therefore right to claim that "I've been here before." The same could be said of all parapraxes: they are mistakes, which is to say that they reflect a facet of unconscious meaning whose "out of placeness" is, after all, what gives them their essential, uncanny identity. The mind is aware, on some level, that the unconscious engines seem to have misfired: there is a subjective sense of mistaken identity, of false perception or expression, even if one is not able to correct it immediately.

A sixty-year-old lawyer in the eighth year of a very productive analysis had a dream in which a parapraxis appeared, the first ever as far as he could remember. A man of keen intelligence and rigorous curiosity, he found that the appearance of unusual fauna in a dream landscape aroused as much interest as a new sighting in an astronomer's telescope. "I've heard of day's residue," he joked, "but this is not residual—it's functional," and he set to work to decode its meaning. Here is the dream as he reported it.

"I'm walking down a city street—New York, probably. Skyscrapers all around. I am walking with Nelson Mandela, but I am calling him Tomás Magadin in error."

In the dream, the error does not seem to generate any anxiety, but on waking, the dreamer is struck by the parapraxis and puzzled by its meaning. The analysand noted that Lord Nelson was an admiral who won a famous sea battle by placing a telescope to his blind eye, therefore not seeing how outnumbered he was, and his ultimate victory proved that blind courage is sometimes more effective than cold-blooded visual reality. "An ambiguous ideal, to say the least," chortled the analysand, impressed by the double-edged wish embodied in the condensation of Nelson the blind and Nelson the victorious. Mandela seemed to pick up the same theme almost in the same breath. Mandela was man with the feminine appendage Della (as in Della Hopkins, a childhood sweetheart of the analysand). Hopkins led to an association to Gerard Manley Hopkins, the innovative poet who introduced the concepts of sprung rhythm and inscape into modern poetry. And the poet's name seemed to condense the manly and the feminine. (The analysand thought of poetry as an expression of feminine aspects of the psyche.)

The dreamer's genetic context needs to be summarized before the dream can be discussed further. As mentioned earlier, the analysand was a sixty-year-old lawyer nearing the end of analysis; he was the product of a white, Anglo-Saxon, Protestant family, in which a powerful mother had steered the family's "ship of state" throughout a lifelong illness of the father, with her son (the analysand) beside her at the wheel. His considerable career and social successes were thus forever tinged with oedipal guilt. In fact, the analysis in large part was an attempt to rescue him from the wreck of success, given his unconscious tendency to undermine himself upon reaching his goals.

Returning to the dream with these bare bones of a genetic sketch, let us attempt further deconstruction while not losing sight of the parapraxis and its function in the dream. Tomás Magadin was the substitute name for Nelson Mandela in the dream. Why Tomás Magadin? The analysand's older brother, Tommy, had cardiac failure at a relatively early age. The analysand was angry and disappointed that his father and brother were not made of sturdier stuff. Magadin was not too dissimilar from the analyst's name, and thus, illness was being wished upon the analyst via transference. "Better you than them," he quipped. "Blood is thicker than water." Magadin elicited the further associations of "maggots in" (symbolic of death) and of the Magi (three wise kings bringing gifts to his royal highness, the baby)—the latter a regressive, compensatory wish in the face of so much death and castration.

Following these associative leads, the analysand had enough information to probe deeper. The eight years of prior analytic work were, of course, the most profound day's residue for this analysand, whose memory was quite remarkable: "Long day's residue into night" was an expression he often applied to the analysis, with characteristic sarcasm. The analysis of bisexual conflicts, for instance, had undergone profound revisions from the first year of the analysis to the eighth: whereas the early years of analysis had been full of heterosexual protest, bisexuality in the eighth year was a topic that aroused curiosity and interest rather than anxiety.

The concept of resolving a conflict with its negative oedipal or preoedipal solutions made the analysand marvel at the variety of his options, rather than doubt the solidity of his sexual identity. Given this newfound comfort with the multiple determinants of heterosexual and homosexual tendencies, the play of ambiguities in the dream puzzled him. If he wanted to be castrated and heroic all at once, like the black phoenix Nelson Mandela, who had leaped from the flames of apartheid and incarceration to be born again as the leader of his people, why could the name Nelson Mandela not stand on its own terms in his dream—as a multiply condensed compromise between defeat and victory, between the blindness of Lord Nelson and the unrelenting vision of Mandela? Why confuse the issue with Tomás Magadin? Why drag in a slip of the tongue to a well-orchestrated dream landscape?

At this point, the analysand had the intriguing insight that Tomás Magadin/Nelson Mandela was not a slip of the tongue in the sense that parapraxes of everyday life are examples of faulty functioning (Fehlleistung). On the contrary, excellence of functioning was being demonstrated as the dream-work pulled out all the stops in the service of disguise. The dreamer's bemusement on awakening that a slip had appeared in his dream was a measure of the success of this red herring in throwing him off the scent of the dream's latent meaning.

Tomás Magadin was not a slip, an error, but a profound association in its own right, as the dreamer's association to Tomás revealed: Tomás sounded like no más, the infamous words of Roberto Durán in his boxing match with Sugar Ray Leonard. Durán refused to continue the fight, throwing in the towel with the words "no más"—no more—a great humiliation for the legendary boxer. Tomás Magadin and its associative siblings, "no más" and "maggots in," were protests against the death of the analysand's brother or the death of the analyst, but behind the protests lay a death wish against both. "I'm glad I'm alive" was the dream's major message. "I'm glad others are dying, not I—make no mistake about it." The bold starkness of the wish had to be concealed in ambiguities and compromises, as if the guilty dreamer could be heroic in his defiance of death and his wishing it on others only when he embraced death and life together in a bisexual compromise! He could not be simply Nelson Mandela in the dream; he needed to cover up this heroic, phallic identity with a more castrated alter ego, Tomás Magadin. And he needed to pretend it had all been a mistake!

When James Joyce (1922) said, "A man of genius makes no mistakes. His errors are volitional and are the portals of discovery" (p. 190), he was talking about Shakespeare and, none too modestly, perhaps, about himself, but he could have been referring to the mind in general: its mistakes, as I have demonstrated in regard to parapraxes in dreams, can be recycled by the dream-work, their form and content pushed into defensive service, as the mind loses no opportunity to enhance the complexity of its disguises. The dream interpreter armed with these insights has an additional strategy at hand with which to keep pace with the magical sleight of hand of dream-work!

8

A TRICK IN A DREAM

In this chapter I focus on an elaborate trick the dream-work has conceived and put on display in manifest content the better to conceal the latent mischief from scrutiny altogether. Let me describe the dream.

> The dreamer and his accomplice are staging a trick for a small audience. Three coins are hidden by the accomplice (whose role as accomplice is known only to the dreamer, not to the audience). The coins are made of gold, silver, and lead, which makes them immediately recognizable when discovered. The dreamer, who in fact does not know where the coins have been hidden, has no trouble pretending to find them since he has similar coins secreted in his pockets. When he "finds" the hidden coins, it is actually these coins, retrieved slyly from his pockets, that he is finding, much to the amazement of his audience. Then the scene shifts to an outdoor location. The dreamer is now cleaning litter from his lawn, which is an elaborate piece of property beside the sea. There is a long rectangular table on the lawn at which his seventy-five-year-old friend and his friend's daughter are seated. He plans to join them as soon as he has collected all the litter in his voluminous black garbage bag.

The analysis of this dream over the next several sessions was most productive. But some context is required to orient the reader to the spirit of the analysis that produced this dream.

Jason (let us call him) was a fifty-year-old economist when the analysis began. His father had died suddenly at age fifty when Jason was fifteen, and consequently his age was fraught with emotional significance for him. His motivation to seek analysis was a reflection of other factors, to be sure, but his concerns about his health, his constitutional endowment, how "the shadow" of his father's life and death, as he called it, had fallen across his own, needed to be assessed. He was an insightful man and was aware, or became aware quickly in the investigative atmosphere of psychoanalysis, of how identified he was with both parents. His mother's tendency to criticize her husband was an unanalyzed idolatry of her own father, in whose shadow all other men failed miserably by comparison. The transference could quickly assume an attitude of contempt toward or denigration of the analyst, mirroring this attitude of his mother toward his father. On a deep, almost unspeakable level, Jason felt that his mistrust of his mother was at the root of another significant reason for entering analysis: he had never married despite a great desire to do so. Relationships seemed to flourish at first but then inevitably faltered and failed. He felt inevitably disappointed and in a somewhat paranoid mood could feel "tricked," as if the fault were not a shared responsibility but a wound inflicted on him by the other. "Look what you've done to me" was the attitude at first until he eventually became more self-reflective and could look at his own part in the failed relationship. He knew his sensitivities were a problem that could make him feel wounded, avoidant, and self-protective, when in fact there was hurt on both sides that needed to be addressed more maturely. His identification with his father, whom he loved deeply, could trigger masochistic, self-destructive tendencies, when survivor guilt demanded suffering and tortured enactments as opposed to cherished

126

memories. Teasing apart the adaptive aspects of these identifications from their pathological components was a major analytic consideration over the years. The topic is vast and can be addressed only briefly here: to the extent that the analysis of the unconscious components of identifications takes years of analytic labor, the surface of a complete explication of all the issues can only be scratched en passant. I am suggesting that the differentiation between a maladaptive, self-destructive identification with mother or father may need to be vigorously addressed, whereas the identification with mother's or father's adaptive attributes, generosity of spirit, for instance, can be investigated less urgently perhaps. (In the final analysis all aspects need deconstruction, of course.) These issues were often on the analysand's mind, especially when he had somatic concerns, and he had trouble sorting out hypochondria from appropriate alertness to essential somatic signals that needed medical attention. At the time of the analysis of the dream in question, he was experiencing palpitations, which were being studied medically by his internist, who was also a cardiologist. His seventy-five-year-old friend (mentioned in the dream) seemed to have no medical problems at all, nor did his analyst. This envy of the analyst's supposed perfect health was concealed until analysis of the transference exposed it. There was genuine affection for the analyst also, of course: comparing our two professions, economy and psychoanalysis, he would sometimes slyly say, "We're both in risk management!" This was typical of his engaging sense of humor. With this brief clinical sketch as guide, let us approach the dream again and consider how analysis eventually exposed its clever tricks and concealments.

The analysand was immediately struck by the elaborate nature of the trick. "My mother used to call my father 'trick-o'-the-loop' when she was angry at him." He went on to explain that in his youth his father had dabbled in amateur magical acts. The mother was drawn to magic also. In her childhood she remembered the fairs that would assemble annually in her town. There were many performing acrobats and jugglers and a trick-o'-the-loop man. He explained the nature of the trick as his mother had described it to him: A belt was wrapped around a snagging pencil-like instrument. Eventually, the belt would be transformed into a figure eight design and the trickster would invite his audience to identify the initial loop, the snagging instrument still in place as a marker. A discerning eye would be convinced that the primal loop around which all the subsequent loops encircled like ripples could be identified and the prize could be claimed. The trick of course was that the trickster could always unleash the belt from its many looped shape in such a way that the original loop would never be snagged by the inserted instrument and the "sucker" who had fallen for the trick would lose his money! So his mother calling his father a trick-o'-the-loop was not a term of endearment. Indeed, when Jason remembered the parental altercations, it still made him nervous, as if his own self-assertive nature was still compromised by these conflicted, ambivalent identifications.

That was the analysand's first association. More associations followed in rapid succession. His envy of the seventy-five-year-old friend's good health led to questions about why he had introduced the friend's daughter into the dream. This made him think about the daughter's obvious oedipal attachment to her robust father. By comparison, he felt diminished, as if his concerns about his heart reflected neurotic anxiety rather reasonable concern about his somatic health. In that context he thought of *The Merchant of Venice* and the possessive father who arranged the three casket "trick" as a way of never having to surrender his Portia to a husband, given that he could count on the narcissism of men to always choose the gold or silver casket as emblems of their own worthiness rather than the lowly lead they would automatically feel was beneath them. In fact, Jason wondered if he himself were not a male version of Portia, "tricked" by his identifications with his parents into an inhibition of his own marital ambitions, his vision of object relations as inherently treacherous, a pathological conviction he was trying to disabuse himself of in the psychoanalytic process.

Jason had never married, although he had come close several times but, as mentioned earlier, he always found a neurotic way out of the commitment. It was when friends pointed this neurotic pattern out to him that he sought analysis. He was developing a most promising relationship with a colleague at the time of reporting the dream, and he wondered what connection there might be between the two phenomena. Further associations confirmed the assumption that relationships never "work." Why am I not at the table with my friend and his daughter? he wondered. He sensed that there was some hostility, some social rudeness, in his not joining them at the breakfast table and also some concealed hostility in the enormous black garbage bag he was stuffing with litter. A body bag came to mind. He thought of dead soldiers returning home in body bags. Did he want to kill his friend and run off with his daughter? Was the daughter an obvious disguise for his friend's wife? Recently he had noticed a woman waiting outside the analyst's office and had imagined that she was the analyst's wife. He had quickly averted his eyes as they glanced at each other. "She's too young for him," he mused as he imagined the analyst's age and the considerably younger woman outside my office. "She's more my age," he dared to consider, then abandoned that line of thinking, since it made him so anxious. That led to a consideration of the accomplice in the dream. Did it represent an unconscious relationship with his mother as accomplice in the trick that was being played on the father? Secretly he was married to his mother, an unholy dyadic alliance that had dispatched the weak father. Such associations led to tears and a sense of guilt that represented itself more as somatic pain than as felt affect. This led to ideas about his identification with his father not only in life but also in death. He wondered if all of his previously failed relationships with women were a reflection of anxiety and guilt, as if he had actually given his father the heart attack that killed him. Was there a perverse loyalty to a dead man at the root of his inertia with women? Many of these themes had been the subject of analysis in the preceding months before the dream was reported, but now the associations visited them all anew and more viscerally. While the family was worried about the father's health and eventual death, the garden in front of the family home was often untended and became littered with papers for a period of time. Such litter was associated with mourning in Jason's mind: in the dream litter and body bag, refuse and death seemed to share an eerie association. "Am I mourning all over in this dream?" he asked. The answer seemed to be yes in the sense that Jason, by regressing to this anal preoccupation with litter and body bags, was absenting himself from the table of his own robust life. "The trick's on me," he said with sardonic humor that was very characteristic of him.

Some of his associations were less negative. The three coins in the dream brought to mind the old movie *Three Coins in the Fountain,* in which three women visiting Rome throw coins in the Trevi Fountain, the tradition being that this magically leads to marital consummation and fulfillment.

A few weeks later Jason had another dream, which he introduced by saying it was a dream with "more trickery in it."

I am seated at a table with an old friend, George, a trusted colleague of mine in the world of economics. To my left is a business associate, a colleague also but not as intimate. He is asking incredulously why am I consorting with my old friend since he is such a persona non grata in academic circles. I am troubled by this disclosure and move away from the table to find another place to seat myself but not without some guilt that I am not sticking up for my friend. At the new table some colleagues say I should go on YouTube and get a subrimeter. In the dream the word seemed to mean something functional.

Upon awakening, Jason is struck by the strange word "subrimeter," which he calls "real word-trickery" and is totally baffled by its meaning. Free associating to the dream content he cites an immediate day's residue: his close colleague and friend George had just sent him a critique of his recent book on economics, which he put aside angrily after reading the first paragraph, which he thought was tentative in its praise. When he read the whole review the next day, he was genuinely surprised by how positive the review was and not a little ashamed of his paranoid reaction. "But the paranoia invaded the dream," he admitted as he worked on the various images in the dream's manifest content. He was ashamed of his disloyalty to his friend, a quality he had "inherited" from his mother, an identification he was trying to rework and revise in the analytic process. His association to "YouTube" was fascinating and creative: "YouTube" sounded to him like "et tu, Brute," modernized as "You tooB(rutus)." "I feel like Brutus when I identify with my mother's fickle nature," he commented. But what Jason called word-trickery got even more puzzling when he turned his free-associative attention to the word "subrimeter." He had just looked up the meaning of "tromometer," whose function is to measure seismic rumblings underground. Could subrimeter be a gadget for measuring subconscious rumblings—the depth psychology beneath the brim of the mind? Or a gadget for detecting the subprime mortgage fiasco before it happened? "I could've used such a gadget and saved the world [from] a disaster," he said, laughing. His mind went back to the trick-o'-the-loop in the earlier dream. "The whole subprime mortgage scandal was a real trick-o'-the loop piece of irresponsible fiscal trickery, a bubble waiting to burst and bring down the whole financial world with it." (Jason had actually been one of the courageous few who cautioned management about reckless risk taking that went beyond the usual bounds of safety and due diligence.) "But I guess it's mental economy we're studying," he said as he turned his attention back to the analysis. The deepest insight he extracted from the dream-work's trickery was the idea that his wish for a gadget—a subrimeter—to plumb the depths of the unconscious would make the analyst unnecessary. "I wouldn't need you," he said. "Et tu, Brute," the analyst said in the role of the stricken Caesar. Jason, struck by the analyst's quick and comfortable assumption of the role he had been so disguisedly assigned, agreed genuinely, and his aggression, flushed out into the open by his insightful analytic probing, seemed safer than ever. His mind went back to the Trevi Fountain, his promising new relationship that was developing staying power, even as he also joked that the three coins in the fountain were a safer financial bet than all the recent market gambles!

Analytic process would indeed eventually strengthen Jason's newfound ability to work in a relationship and make it last. He overcame his phobia of commitment and married the woman he loved. He learned to decipher dream trickery as a convoluted, distorted, fearful kind of communication that nevertheless had really useful information embedded in it if you put in the hours of analytic work decoding it. Subrimeters could help you go deep if you saw through their unconscious trickery.

What can be added to Jason's insightful analysis of these issues? A developmental and genetic point of view can augment these insights. To the extent that every child's exclusive love of the mother in the early dyadic climate of the first one or two years of life suffers a rude awakening when triadic conflict and the Oedipus complex assume and assert their prominence from three to five approximately, every child must feel as if a nasty trick has been played on him. It must feel as if the idealized mother suddenly declared the primacy of her relationship with her husband, much to the horror of her jilted lover. The child tries to maintain a dyadic relationship with each parent to the exclusion of the rivalrous other, in positive and negative oedipal variations on this tormented theme. Having to negotiate the Oedipus complex must feel like a trick being played on the child, a trick that never leads to a satisfactory conclusion. The only solution is compromise: the child eventually (usually around six years of age) represses his love and hatred toward his treacherous parents, identifies with their authority, and waits to find his own exclusive mate many years later. But the sense that nature has built a trick into its developmental design leaves a bitter taste forever.

The three coins in the dream brought *The Merchant of Venice* to Jason's mind, the gold, silver, and lead coins bearing a relationship to the gold, silver, and lead caskets in the celebrated play. In his paper "The Theme of the Three Caskets," Freud (1913) argued that the three caskets are a disguised representation of the Three Sisters, "the Fates, the Moerae, the Parcae or the Norns, the third of whom is called Atropos, the inexorable" (p. 296). He compared them also to Lear's three daughters, whom Freud believed were a disguised representation of death. (In "A Note on 'The Theme of the Three Caskets,'" I argued that Freud's ambivalent death wishes toward Jung were the unconscious or preconscious triggers of that paper. I cited evidence from Schur's biography of Freud that suggested the paper was written just after Freud had visited an ailing Binswanger in Kreuzlingen but had not visited the nearby Jung at the time, which Jung took as a slur against him, later referring to it as the "Kreuzlingen Incident.") The rift, which would eventually doom the Freud–Jung relationship, was widening irrevocably at this point in time. This interesting aside into the nature of Freud's creativity would take us too far afield from the discussion at hand. Suffice it to say that death wishes were on Freud's mind as he put pen to paper in 1912, just as they seem to have been on Jason's mind as the dream-work set about to concoct its disguises.

In the manifest content of the dream, the dreamer triumphs since he has rigged the trick in his favor. Nature, by designing the inevitable triangle at the core of procreation, seemed to be tricking human beings with a confounding Oedipus complex, a riddle that could never be solved. Oedipus himself in mythology had defeated the Sphinx by cracking the code of a most oedipal riddle, which depicts the rise of man from all fours as an infant to upright, two-footed toddler and subsequent manhood status only to be demeaned again as a three-legged old man who needs to support his two shaky legs with a third (the walking stick). The word "imbecile" before it took on its nineteenth-century meaning of feeble-minded at first meant feeble-bodied or weak limbed, literally as frail as an old man without a staff (from Latin "in-baculum," meaning "without a staff"). By rigging the trick in his favor, the dreamer, at least in his manifest triumph, is fooling Mother Nature at her own game. Freud's favorite misquotation was Falstaff's "Thou owest God a debt," which Freud quoted as "Thou owest Nature a debt" on a few occasions, Freud's atheism dictating the terms of the parapraxis, no doubt. In Jason's latent content, the dream thoughts may well have been: "I know I must, out of loyalty to the father I killed unconsciously, identify with his suffering and death, thereby becoming the gull of my own neurotic trick. Even if I seem to have the terms of the trick figured out in my favor in the manifest content, I will also include a scene in the manifest display in which I am a regressed anal litter gatherer while the oedipal man and woman dine at the table without me. Even if I let myself triumph over fools with the cleverness of my trick, the coins will also represent the death I carry around with me concealed in my pockets like three fatal caskets."

From a genetic point of view, Jason's regression to litter gatherer in the dream echoes the original childhood solution to the Oedipus complex as Freud imagined it. Not only are repression, infantile amnesia, and identification called upon to solve the oedipal dilemma, but regression is also necessary: the oedipal configuration regresses to an anal retreat, an infantile messiness, that the ego then transforms into obsessional defense mechanisms, thereby explaining the rather rigid defensive structure of latency. In child analysis one can see this remarkable transformation in statu nascendi: a playful, fantasy-ridden oedipal child becomes a more rigid, industrious, intellect-driven, and cognitively advanced latency child—not overnight, of course, but quite dramatically nonetheless as the child ages from a five-year-old into a six- or seven-year-old.

Of course the transference and its interpretation are other features of analytic process that lend themselves to being misconstrued as "tricks." What analysand does not feel "tricked" on some level when s/he imagines that the analyst is saying that the love or the hate engendered in the analytic process is not "real" since it is a transformation in the form of transference from a more primal, genetic source? Perhaps the greatest "trick" of all is the dream-work's sorcery: through the ministry of primary processes, it transforms latent dream thoughts into a disguised, fantastic version of themselves, a metamorphosis that Bottom, in *A Midsummer Night's Dream*, captures well when he says, "I have had a dream, past the wit of man to say what dream it was." It is hard not to feel tricked when one awakens from a dream that has been constructed so cunningly and deceptively out of primary processes that the awakener has no access to, unless he subjects the dream to a psychoanalytic method that tries to follow myriad free-associative clues back to the blueprints of a crafty architect (the dream-work) who covers his tracks so cleverly and confoundingly. It is hard to get to the bottom of a dream that Bottom says "hath no bottom." It is only when we realize that Jason's trick in the manifest content of his dream is already a clever transformation, orchestrated by primary processes I am calling the dream-work's trick that we can approach the bottomless meanings at all. The manifest trick must lead the awakened dreamer to the original dream-work trick using the psychoanalytic method as guide. Apropos the bottom of a dream, Freud's comment would seem to be the crucial one: "At bottom, dreams are nothing other than a particular *form* of thinking, made possible by the conditions of the state of sleep. It is the *dream-work* which creates that form, and it alone is the essence of dreaming—the explanation of its peculiar nature" (Freud, 1900, p. 506–7).

Without a knowledge of the dream-work's incredible inventiveness, or esthetic trickery, dreams do seem to be bottomless and unfathomable.

If we assume that the original dream thoughts were incestuous or murderous and were leading to nightmarish fears of abandonment, loss of love, castration—the hierarchy of calamities Freud outlined, in other words—their transformation into a clever, if psychopathic trick, seems to have the function of assuring the dreamer that loss, as a consequence of the possessive sexual conquest of mother or murderous assault on the father, need never be feared. The trick assures the trickster that he will never be at a loss. The dream-work's direction and production of the manifest movie montage is so impressive, the dreamer and even the awakener might never think of digging deeper for the dream thoughts that have been so utterly changed into such arresting images. The dream-work's trickery in the subrimeter dream would seem to be of a different order entirely. The awakener is bound to have his curiosity whetted by how bewildered he is by the neologism. But his curiosity will be unrewarded unless he applies the psychoanalytic method with great intensity. Jason was a most insightful analysand and even took YouTube to be analytic fair game for a clever dissection that exposed the murderous wish in its disguise of "et tu, Brute." Similarly, it was damnably clever of Jason to dig the subprime mortgage crisis out of subrimeter, not to mention its identity as a gadget for exploring depth psychology that would make the presence of the analyst unnecessary. Again the death wish toward the analyst was masterfully disguised. Intense condensation would seem to be the dream-work's main ally in the construction of the neologism. Displacement and representation of unconscious dream thoughts pictorially and dramatically seem to be the chief architects of the "three-coin trick" dream, however.

It is interesting to think of the dream-work as a master tactician, a most sophisticated trickster who has turned deception itself into a fine art. It is impossible not to think of it as other than a most advanced ego function that the sleeping brain retains in a state of acute alertness despite its unconscious form. It is akin to creativity itself and its access to preconscious states that make a work of art so uncannily relevant and beautiful despite the baffling indirectness of the communication. The way dream-work transforms a latent dream thought into such distortions and disguises of itself that recognition becomes impossible can be compared to the mastery of a jazz musician, perhaps, who can take a simple melody from the Great American Songbook—or any other songbook, for that matter—and put it through such improvised metamorphoses of itself that the ear has trouble retaining the original melody in mind as the variations riff on and on so dazzlingly and dizzyingly. The melody is changed utterly as improvisation struts its stuff and beauty is born on the spot like a dream.

In terms of Jason's problems with commitment to human relationships that cannot be controlled with trickery but must be entered into wholeheartedly, the seduction of the trick represented the appeal of regressive magic when reality seemed a game that was too hard to enter into without a few tricks up your sleeve. He was working hard in his analysis to fight against these regressive tendencies. The dream depicted his conflicts very dramatically. Remembering the dreams and working on them with his considerable intelligence represented the triumph of insight over the seductions of trickery. He was choosing what Freud called the "slow magic" (Whitebook, 2002) of psychoanalytic process over the processes of the seemingly fast-acting magic trickery of self-deception.

9

A JOKE IN A DREAM

If a dream can "pretend" to embed another dream within the artistry of its own disguise, confounding the awakener with the virtuosity of its sleeping sleight-of-handedness, we now pursue this irony of a sleeping ego that seems to be wide awake in the middle of the night, weaving layers and layers of manifest imagery, with the purpose of completely hiding latent meanings. This time an embedded joke rather than a dream is our topic. Freud believed that jokes in dreams were not really "formally" successful, the dream-work exploiting them with "defensive" rather than "comic" intent. Now I want to present the content of a dream in which the embedded joke was actually "funny" by esthetic standards. It did conform to the usually acceptable standards of joke telling in real as opposed to oneiric time. We now turn our attention to why the dream-work employed this unusual technique and the dynamic reasons for such an extra flourish of disguise in the midst of what is, after all, a pretty elaborate concoction of disguises already.

> I go to a restaurant. You [the analyst] are there too with your wife. Suddenly I bite my tongue. You [the analyst] say, "Oh, at least one of us will have a good meal." Paul Newman is in the restaurant also, and I comment, "Oh, he comes here too."

The analyst was immediately struck not only by the sarcastic piece of comic humor that had been assigned to his persona in the dream but also by how genuinely funny the structure of the dream joke seemed. It was not a dream joke that "leaves us cold" and "does not make us laugh" as Freud had suggested. This is true of most dreams: if the comic appears in a dream, it is merely part of the whole mise-en-scène. Its function is not to amuse but to further disguise like all the other manifest components. But there are exceptions, as the dream I have just described illustrates. It seemed to be an example of a true joke, exploited no doubt by the dream-work in the service of disguise, a piece of dream text that would not reveal its meanings until the free-associative processes of dream interpretation made sense out of its opacities as well as of what seemed to be its transparencies. While the analyst was genuinely amused by the perverse laughter the joke seemed to elicit, he was also aware of the analytic challenge of a piece of humor that seemed to celebrate sadism's comic triumph over misery's self-inflicted wounds. The "good meal" the dream joke celebrates was, after all, a swallowing of one's own flesh, the self its own totem meal in a piece of savage cannibalistic self-sacrifice. Was masochism ever better captured symbolically than in this caricature of nourishment, horror masquerading as humor as the self makes a meal of the self?

The dreamer's analytic context must be cited in an attempt to bring coherence to a piece of clinical material that has been presented so precipitously without associative or genetic background. The dreamer is a forty-five-year-old architect who had recently received a significant commission that would prove to be a turning point in his career, financially and artistically. He was the younger of two siblings in a highly successful artistic family (mother a successful novelist, brother a renowned musician). His own success seemed more conflicted given his identification with a depressed father whose career as a writer never amounted to what early promise seemed to have assured. This identification and a sadistic superego that seemed to accompany it became the main focus of an analysis that was most productive and nearing termination when the dream under discussion jolted the dreamer with its wry sarcasm and arresting ironies.

In the next several sessions, the main themes beneath the manifest content of the dream slowly revealed themselves. The analysand was a nail biter for the first twenty years of his life. Oral issues were often prominent as free-associative process and genetic recall gave shape to his childhood conflicts. The biting of the tongue in the dream was a reprise of an ancient oral sadomasochistic assault on his own flesh, self-punishment a defense against a complex dialogue of love and hate with mother, father, and brother. Identification with a successful mother and a castrated father created a dual internal conflicted imagery that was confounding when oedipal issues were being processed. Regression to masochistic oral imagery of auto castration (biting his own tongue) seemed safer than competitive displays of castration wishes toward a father who might not be able to "take it," given the already dilapidated state of his self-esteem. This old genetic theme was very much alive in the transference neurosis, as the dream imagery suggests. The dream arena is a restaurant that Newman, a "new man," frequents. The patient's new identity as successful architect and successful analysand occupies one pole of the dream, while auto castration dominates the other pole, the analyst's endorsement of the neurotic resolution cloaked in humor. For many sessions, in fact, the analyst's sarcasm in the dream was experienced as if the dream were factual rather than a product of dream-work. The idea that the analysand's success could "finish off" the father or "finish off" the analyst (one meaning of the termination phase) needed the massive reversal implied by the biting of the tongue. The dream joke, in other words, was a would-be collusion between a hoped-for countertransferential analyst who would "celebrate" the analysand's self-destructive neurosis rather than analyze it. The "collusion" had genetic roots, of course, in the childhood fantasy that the patient and his mother had successfully "finished off" the father, a piece of unconscious mental imagery that was exciting and terrifying all at once. It would be "fun" to get away with "murder," neurosis seems to suggest, but the joke is on the neurotic in the sense that one doesn't get away with the imaginary crime at all but suffers forever as if one had! Neurosis is a bad joke against the self that the neurotic acts out without realizing the tragicomic drama in which he is trapped. As these issues became even more obvious in the analytic process, the "function" of the joke in the dream became more accessible. The analysand, well informed by this stage of analysis about the basic components and strategies of dream disguise, was able to ponder the unusual appearance in a dream of a joke that would have seemed funny even in waking life.

10

A PUN IN A DREAM

From humor in a dream we turn to yet another example of dream-work virtuosity: the appearance of a pun in a dream, a pun that concealed half of its meaning from the dreamer but revealed it to the astonished awakener, who eventually made very good use of the insight. In this section of a chapter that deals with dreams from a variety of novel viewpoints, I am trying to emphasize again the cunning of the dream-work as it selects what it needs to fulfill infantile wishes, using the most beguiling disguises.

Mr. J, a professor of English literature, in analysis for many years, recently reported the following dream:

> I am at the closing of a real estate transaction. All the parties are assembled around an official-looking table in a typical room of a bank or some such institution. The lawyers are present, but the deal cannot go through because the didn'ter isn't present.

The strange word "didn'ter" seemed to make sense in the dream, as if the didn'ter were as expectable a presence as the lawyers or bank officials who attend closings. "Didn'ter" was pronounced in the dream like "didn't" (the contracted form of did not) with an "er" attached to it, turning the verb into a noun. Initially, Mr. J did not recognize the pun that didn'ter concealed. When he did, he was jolted: didn'ter, with a slight change in pronunciation, became did inter, meaning did bury the body.

The verb "inter" had been on the analysand's mind for two very significant reasons: (1) He had just reread Shakespeare's *Julius Caesar* (1599), and the lines "The evil that men do lives after them;/The good is oft interred with their bones" (III, 2, 75–76) had jolted him as if he had just read them for the first time. (2) A friend had just died and was buried the day before Mr. J had this dream.

Further associations eventually made it possible to reconstruct the latent dream thoughts that the dream-work had disguised in the manifest content. Mr. J's friend was buried in his hometown, a village called New Place. The analysand knew that New Place was also the name of the house Shakespeare had acquired in Stratford-upon-Avon after he became famous and prosperous. Mr. J began to sense that the coincidental irony of two New Places had been co-opted by the dream-work while the unconscious scaffolding of the dream was being constructed. In playing free-associatively with the manifest content, it became clear that not only was a closing being stalled because the didn'ter was not present, but also the alternative meaning, did inter, was being concealed lest the reality of the burial of his friend be exposed.

On deeper reflection, it became clear that it was not just the reality of the burial that was being denied: the psychological reality of Mr. J's death wishes toward his friend was even more objectionable. The analysand had visited his friend in the hospital just prior to his death, when he was semi-comatose and close to the end. Mr. J left the hospital with a great sense of sadness and a great sense of his own mortality and how tenuous the human lease of life seemed upon reflection on occasions such as these. He was not aware of how angry he was with his friend for reminding him to "ask not for whom the bell tolls," since "it tolls for thee." Nor was he aware of how happy he was to be alive and how happy he was that it was his friend who was dying and not he.

When his friend did die a day later, Mr. J became aware of his sense of paralysis and deadness—as if he, too, had died, or at least would do so very soon. This "identification" with his friend reminded him of how deeply he had been identified with his own father since childhood. Like Mr. J himself, his father had been a professor of English literature, but alcoholism had destroyed his academic career as well as his social life. His wife finally left him after trying for years to put up with his exasperating behavior, but the analysand was aware that he himself had never left him, so profound was the ambivalent identification with him. The death of Mr. J's friend stirred up all these issues, which had been the daily subject matter of analysis for many years.

As mentioned, when he learned that his friend was to be buried in his childhood village of New Place, Mr. J was reminded of Shakespeare's ownership of a house of the same name. What would not become conscious until the analysis of the dream was more complete, however, was the wish to usurp the place of his friend and the place of his father (not to mention the usurpation of the literary status of the father of all playwrights, William Shakespeare!), and to make his oedipal conquest permanent by carving *his name only* on the new place.

Ironically, the word "assassination" makes its first entrance as a verbal entity in the English language in *Julius Caesar*, a play that had recently captured Mr. J's attention, as noted—especially the line "the good is oft interred with their bones." The analysand was all too aware that the evil men do or feel not only "lives after them" but also lives with them, no matter how desperately they attempt to conceal it. These kinds of ruminations, self-accusations, and free associations led eventually to an understanding of the latent dream thoughts and how the pun had become a useful sop for the dream-work to employ in keeping an unwitting Cerberus (the dream censor) beguiled.

Many sessions of analytic process made it clear that the latent dream thoughts were stark, oedipal, acquisitive designs to plunder "the old man's" estate once death had "closed" his eyes permanently! The dreamer, after years of analysis, was quite familiar with the "professorial" ego style that shaped the manifest content not only of his character but of his dreams as well. The "gift" of a "literary" dream with which to seduce the "intellectual" analyst is a transference-countertransference issue of no small importance, but I want to focus almost exclusively on one aspect of dream-work, which Mr. J came to appreciate over time. As compressed and polished as his impressive character traits and defenses were, he came to realize that the unconscious compression of his own dream-work was a marvel of condensed meanings as well, meanings that had eluded him earlier.

In the dream under discussion, for instance, as Mr. J's free associations opened his eyes to the many meanings of "closing," the analytic process edged its way toward the hidden meaning embedded in "didn'ter." What began as bemused puzzlement upon awakening, as the dream and its strange new word left the nocturnal realm to enter consciousness, was transformed into the insight that removed the mask from "didn'ter" to reveal "did inter" instead. This could not have been accomplished had Mr. J's ego not become more and more comfortable, over years of analytic process, with the recognition of its own murderous wishes—a revelation that transference, and its ongoing interpretation, had largely made possible. It was the gains of analysis, and the attendant expansion of the ego, that allowed the analysand to deconstruct the dream-work's compressions and put the unconscious energies to alternative, adaptive uses.

After an awakener has analyzed such a dream and fully appreciated the complexity of its wordplay, he perhaps cannot help feeling like Alice in her puzzling conversation with Humpty Dumpty about the words "glory" and "impenetrability." In this celebrated passage (Carroll, 1872, pp. 238–239), when Alice challenges Humpty Dumpty's definition of "glory," Humpty Dumpty says, "When I use a word, it means just what I choose it to mean— neither more nor less." Later, when Humpty Dumpty explains the word "impenetrability" to her in a complicated way, Alice says, "That's a great deal to make one word mean." Humpty Dumpty explains: "When I make a word do a lot of work like that, I always pay it extra."

If the dream-work behind the dream described here can be compared to the inscrutable Humpty Dumpty, perhaps we can assume that it paid the word "didn'ter" quite a bit extra for all the work it made it do.

147

11

A CARTOON IN A DREAM

A cartoon in a dream is an unusual example of an "inclusion body," so to speak, planted in manifest content by the dream-work. In this chapter I focus on a rather vivid cartoon image that took center stage, hoping to keep the focus entirely on manifest content and leave the latent content unexamined even when the awakener begins to analyze the dream.

The dream is described at first, along with three other dreams from the same night, followed by sufficient clinical material to provide context for the dream analysis that is the main topic of this article.

Dream 1

A woman surprises her audience. One was expecting a happy ending, but on the contrary, the woman is sick. Quite sick. So is her accomplice.

Dream 2

The dreamer enters a room where women are giving a lecture. He sees his father on the floor with a mop in his hand. He joins him out of loyalty, out of solidarity. The women are talking about social work or sociology. The dreamer confronts them arrogantly, sarcastically, saying that all social commerce is interactional. If something costs ten dollars, one can still negotiate and offer nine dollars—it's all interactional.

Dream 3

A cartoon appears in a dream. A seascape. Tall mountain or cliff on left of seascape. The beach stretches in a long rectangle to the right of the mountain. There are two groups assembled at the base of the mountain. First group looks conservative; in front of them is a more aggressive group that believes in telling their clients nothing, no matter what Rodrigo, a famous visionary economist, counsels. A line at the bottom of the cartoon, where a caption could be added, is left vacant.

Dream 4

A Professor Greenhouse asks dreamer if he could pretend to be sick so that instead of presenting his paper to the audience, he would speak for only a minute. The dreamer says: Why on earth would I do that? He then realizes he is not being asked; he is being told.

The dreamer is a highly educated forty-year-old businessman, a renaissance man essentially, who inherited the family business. The business was about to file for chapter 11, however, so recklessly and self-destructively had his father managed his assets. Let us call him Carter, by way of honoring his cartoon. I will try to capture the spirit of the man while disguising his profession and identity significantly. He had a law degree from a prestigious university. But his interests went far beyond business and law given his irrepressible creativity. He dabbled in book publishing, film making, and had started a novel at about the time he entered analysis. He was aware that relationships were very problematic for him despite his natural social charm. He had married once with disastrous results. He knew he needed analysis earlier but found many excuses for not engaging in analytic process sooner. The dreams under review come from mid-analysis. Let me describe his childhood, his genetic development, and a summary of the analysis so that the reader has enough clinical context to understand the dynamics of the dreams.

Carter is an only child. He had often wished for older siblings who might have acted as a buffer between himself and his dysfunctional, sadistic parents. His mother, a socialite, seemed to have rejected her son from birth, as if he were the embodiment of all that she hated in her own mother and brother. There was nothing Carter could do to please her. If he was phallic, exuberant, or assertive, she hated that. Did he not know how much he had just hurt his grandfather by being so cocky? If he acted needy and helpless, she hated his weakness. He characterized it as a soul murder as soon as he was able to articulate such concepts. His father was never around, constantly traveling, supposedly for business reasons, but Carter had always assumed there was more to it than that.

In the transference, my vacations were always experienced as not unlike the betrayals of a father who didn't care or of a mother who meant him harm. Carter was a most curious, psychologically minded man, and analysis was most productive. He could be too polite and charming, and it took work to undo an "unobjectionable part of the transference" (Stein, M., 1981) that he might have basked in forever without analytic interventions.

At the time of the dreams in question, Carter was examining his relationship with his mother and father as well as some business colleagues who were often mistaken for hostile stand-ins for the dysfunctional parents. Another significant issue was Carter's new business: he had "gone out on his own," forming an elite business, which he experienced as a major act of individuation on his part. He expected severe retaliation from his parents for daring to individuate from them. His business interests could

151

consume him, so much so that social life became nonexistent. He was aware or gradually became aware that his constant transference of his noxious relationship with his parents onto all his friends, business associates, and especially women made a social life or a sexual life almost impossible for him. Long-term exegesis of these issues in the analysis began eventually to allow progress in all these areas. Examination of the transference was crucial. He treated me as if I couldn't wait to get rid of him; he was constantly watching the clock so that he would be prepared to leave before I could announce the end of the session. Eventually he was able to laugh at the clock that formerly used to menace him. A session that ran over a few minutes without his noticing marked a major breakthrough in this kind of pathological vigilance. With this minimal sketch of his life and character and attitude in the transference, let us proceed to examine the dreams.

Carter believed all four dreams were intimately related. He spent several days working on them. Dream 1, in which the woman surprises everyone by being sicker than expected, seemed to represent the mother who he had come to realize was indeed "a very sick woman." Her accomplice seemed to represent his father, who had never intervened in some salutary manner to protect his son from her constant sadism. In a sense he was expecting a normal, healthy mother (the average expectable promise of birthright) and was astonished by the actual mother who was unable to cherish and love her only child.

In Dream 2, out of loyalty he joins his father on the floor and speaks rather arrogantly and defiantly against the women who are discussing social work or sociology. He suggests that all social commerce is *interactional*. A ten-dollar price could always be negotiated down to nine dollars: it's *interactional*. Carter experienced both these dreams as if a coiled aggression was about to spring out at the women in both dreams. At this stage of the analysis, Carter had gotten in touch with the ferocity of his affect toward his mother. He was also much more aggressive with me in the transference.

He had remembered some genetic events that were most disturbing. He remembered wanting to draw blood as he bared his teeth at his mother, a fantasy that really frightened him. He became a vegetarian for several years in childhood until the symptom vanished in adolescence. He was a "ferocious athlete" for a number of years in adolescence, an activity, he believed, that may have returned his taste for meat to him by affording him an outlet for bottled-up aggression.

Dream 3 with the cartoon in it is our main topic, so I plan to focus on it most extensively. Carter was very taken with it. He found it most unusual and sensed that it represented some very creative efforts on behalf of what he called the unconscious spinmeisters. He joked: "Ninety percent of *New Yorker* readers look at the cartoons first, and the other ten percent is lying." He had an immediate association to the mountain cliffs and seascape. It reminded him of a scene from a novel—or was it a movie?—in which a woman, having fallen asleep on the beach, is about to be engulfed by the ocean until she notices a vertical cave in the cliff side, which she climbs up and up to safety. At the top there is a monastery, and the nuns, frightened at first but then sensing a divine intervention, welcome the miraculous apparition into their midst. He wondered about the analytic process. Was it too engulfing of late as the raw aggression rose to the surface? Could it destroy parents and analyst in one gulp of the sea's voracious maw? He assumed that the aggressive group on the beach who insisted on sharing nothing with their clients, regardless of what Rodrigo says, represented his own repressions and reaction formations, which at times could shut down the analytic momentum almost entirely. He had become aware that such resistances were part of the analytic work, despite the ferocity with which he could attack himself when he felt he was not being a compliant patient.

He wondered whether Dream 1 and Dream 2 had gotten too close to murderous aggression toward his mother and needed to be shut down in Dream 3 altogether. He was most struck by Rodrigo, and upon awakening, his conviction that Rodrigo was a celebrated economist was unshakable even though Google could not confirm that for him. Even in the dream Rodrigo seemed as well known as Karl Marx or Adam Smith. Then it came to him suddenly that there was a character called Roderigo in *Othello*, which he had just seen in a Shakespeare in the Park production. In the first scene of the play, Iago and his friend Roderigo are trying to incense Brabantio, Desdemona's father, against the Moor Othello. They both say hateful things about the Moor and how even now he is doing "the beast with two backs" with Brabantio's daughter. Carter was aware that his insistence on seeing Rodrigo (without the "e" in the dream) as an economist as opposed to Iago's sidekick in *Othello* must be significant. He wondered if Othello did not represent his mother and Roderigo himself, railing against the beast with two backs (the voracious sexual mother), who in the primal scene had killed his father in an act of brutal intercourse. He realized Othello was nothing like his mother and that perhaps it was his identification with a man who strangles a woman that was more to the point.

He had learned that in dreams he could be all the characters all at once! He then associated to the *interactional* concept in dream 2: Did all interaction seem like a monstrous primal beast-like behavior to him that could explain his inability to "interact" with women in a safe, loving sexual manner? I asked about his interaction with me in the transference. He said that it used to be something to be feared, but that our work on it had made it more human. He had come to believe that he was obsessed with the menacing clock but that I wasn't.

I asked him what thoughts he had about the missing *e* in the dream "Rodrigo"? Could it be *e* for "energy," like in Einstein's $e = mc^2$? he questioned. Was he disavowing his agency, getting rid of his energy, getting rid of his ego? Wasn't there an ego in the sound of "Rodrigo," the supposedly world-famous economist? He could see that there was a conflict in the dream between the forces of the ego (Rodrigo) that believe in communication, as opposed to the group that believes no information should be shared at all. Did he want to be an informed, *interactional* man or an ignorant man who repressed or disavowed powerful affects? Wasn't that the essential conflict of the dream? Professor Greenhouse in Dream 4 must surely be his own sadistic conscience silencing him as it relieved him of the honor of presenting his paper to the assembled audience. "He was not being asked to curtail his statement to a few words: he was being told!" he said mockingly, as if he could see through his own sadism in the dream.

Carter believed that all four dreams were complex associations to one another. The analyst was still puzzled by the introduction of the cartoon into the dream and asked about that. Carter could not speak for the dreamwork's intentionality, obviously; what he did say was that in the dream he felt like he was looking at the bottom of the cartoon to see if the caption was there, but all he could see was the beach and underneath the beach the line that waits for the caption to be filled as in the *New Yorker* Cartoon Caption Contest. Did the expectant caption represent the analyst's potential interpretation of the dream, an appeal for help from a source he had come to trust, a source that did not retaliate against him no matter how biting his sarcasm could be at times? He had one further ingenious association to Professor Greenhouse: a group of business associates had recently been discussing the greenhouse effect in regard to global warming. He had asked why it was called the greenhouse effect but got no satisfactory answer to his question. He thought it had to do with glasshouses or greenhouses that retained their warmth in winter, allowing plants to grow indoors in the winter months. But he had jokingly said to a colleague maybe it had to do with a Professor Greenhouse, who discovered the phenomenon! And so he researched it and discovered that global warming could be compared to a greenhouse in the sense that fuel emissions create a kind of roof far up in the stratosphere that keeps heat from escaping upward and so contributes

155

dangerously to global warming. There is no way Carter could never have known what the greenhouse effect was. In fact, he had researched it a number of times but could never retain the information. It was obvious that he did know what the greenhouse effect was but chose not to know for neurotic reasons.

He associated to his mother as a kind of pathological roof above his development, a kind of glass ceiling that stifled his growth. He knew he had to live with the sadness and trauma of that reality no matter how much the analysis freed him up to be comfortable with the range of his emotions, sexual and aggressive. But despite the intractability of his sense of trauma and murdered soul, that might never heal completely, he had entered into a promising long-term romantic relationship, which was "working" and even if it could not undo the traumas of childhood completely, it could prepare a present tense and a future tense that had no obstructive or destructive limits set on it. Similarly, in the long-term relationship with the analyst, he had grown comfortable wailing about a sense of irreparable childhood despair, as well as expressing fierce aggressive affect toward the person of the analyst whenever he experienced the analyst as not being really able to bear his pain and stay with it without rejecting it out of some countertransferential discomfort with the intensity of it. It's all "interactional," he would say, as if analytic negotiation could always strip toxic neurotic sadomasochistic relating of its regressive grip on reality. A ten could be reduced to a nine through the ministry of analytic negotiation. A ten referred to the highest level of unbearable pain or aggression that could be modified down a notch through interactive analytic communication, thereby becoming manageable.

Carter used his dreams most effectively to gather all the insights they contained and put them to use in his analysis. He was a hardworking, most engaged analysand, and all that remains to say are a few theoretical comments. I have been interested for years in the cunning of the dream-work as it employs its disguises so ingeniously. In what follows I *personify* the dream-work to create a dramatic effect. I have argued that when the dream-work *inserts* a parapraxis—a pun, a joke, a trick, et cetera—in the manifest content of a dream, there must be a compelling defensive reason for doing so. I have tried to imagine that moment, when sexual or aggressive latent dream thoughts are on the verge of bursting undisguisedly onto the stage, as manifest content is failing to assemble its defensive images successfully.

I am picturing manifest content as the result of an act of creation that displays infantile wishes in such a disguised manner that dreamer and censor and even the awakener are all fooled. The dream with all its disguises in place can be dismissed as nothing more than a dream. But what about that moment when nightmarish affect is about to scuttle the whole esthetic mise-en-scène, and awakening, with its flight into reality, is the only escape valve, the only way to save the endangered dreamer from the oneiric danger that has befallen them At such moments of esthetic failure, I imagine the dream-work as impresario pulling out all the stops and introducing a comic relief (in the form of a joke) or a most visual creation such as a cartoon to distract the impending terror from its alarming affect so that dream and defense can proceed to beguile, amuse, confound while sleep continues. I am imagining this as an esthetic issue, not unlike a horror story writer like Edgar Allen Poe or Stephen King titrating just the right amount of horror into a piece of fiction so as to beguile and seduce the reader with the exact amount of horror that will "hook" him or her into the literary flow of the fiction rather than frightening the reader off altogether. Similarly, a dream can play with the combustible elements of latent dream thoughts, but artistry is required so that the whole esthetic effect doesn't blow up in the dreamer's hands and destroy sleep altogether.

In sleep, as Freud ingeniously argued, the usual kind of verbal representation of communicative reality is usurped completely by an almost totally visual parade of images that make dreams so surreal and engaging. Secondary process is tossed aside, so to speak, as primary processes strut their stuff. Dream display is almost totally visual, a total regression from word presentations to illuminated thing presentations, a display of reality so altered by primary processes as to be unintelligible to the awakener unless they are schooled in a Freudian, free-associative methodology that translates manifest disguise back into the latent dream thoughts that engendered them. If we imagine a hole about to form in that manifest firmament as the *ozone* of instinctual pressure damages the roof of illusion, then a most resourceful dream-work may need to plug the hole with a clever stopgap gag or flourish to save the dream from extinction. Enter a cartoon in a dream as such a dream-saving flourish.

A cartoon is usually a visual montage that cries out for a caption to complete it. However, the best cartoons almost need no caption at all, such is the completeness of the visual statement. A cartoon by Sempe or Steig or Steed seems to need no caption at all to assist the visual statement. That said, the caption contest in the *New Yorker* attests to the readers' appetite for the sheer joy of finding just the right word or two to enhance the cartoon or complete it. In terms of dream structure, the manifest content is the cartoon, the caption is the interpretation that teases the condensations apart, retraces the displacements back to their latent origins or sees through the double-talk of symbolism into the unitary meaning that is being obfuscated. The deconstruction of metaphor's condensations so that the two images can be displayed in separate isolation distills dream-work's alchemy into its components.

This too-theoretical discussion can be brought down to earth if we examine the cartoon that appeared in Dream 3. There is a mountain or cliff far to the left of a rectangular space that denotes sea and beach stretching all the way to the right. There are two groups of people on the beach in front of the sheer cliff. One group insists that nothing should be communicated to the clients regardless of what Rodrigo says. One association of the dreamer has to do with a movie or a novel in which a woman about to be engulfed by the sea escapes to safety by climbing up a narrow cave in the cliff to a monastery. Carter was aware that escape from the ferocity of his anger at both parents could not be accomplished through avoidance or disavowal or repression or regressive self-destructive acts. He was aware that his most dangerous acts of violence against himself always had a component of love in them, as if his mother would be forced to interact lovingly with him if he became paralyzed and derelict at her doorstep. This was pure desperation in fantasy, which reality would never redress for him. Escape from his own affects when their torrents seemed to engulf him was often expressed concretely or geographically, as if it would be possible to take a vacation from them through flight or phobic avoidance. He often contemplated relocation to another city, as if a change of location would magically remove his mind from his intrapsychic suffering. It was a crucial insight for him when he learned that such escape was a futile gesture and that processing the affects in the interactional discourse of analysis was the only long-term solution that had any chance of success. A clever cartoon could distract momentarily just as dream could change latent disturbing thoughts into visual transformations; this could beguile or mystify momentarily, but on awakening it was important to engage the challenge of dream instinct and affect more directly, more realistically.

From a theoretical point of view, a cartoon with its heightened visual and yet somewhat cryptic portrayal of itself seems to be a caricature of the usual visual illuminated montage of a dream. The cartoon seeks to upstage the dream's manifest imagery with an even more ostentatious image that grabs all the limelight, as if to outdream the dream, or outshine it. Just as an engaging *New Yorker* cartoon tends to distract from the more serious articles in the periodical, at least initially, so does a dream cartoon attempt to focus all attention on itself away from the disturbing latent raw material. Carter's attention was certainly taken with the cartoon and a possible caption for it, a distraction that took him away from a closer examination of the many other dreams he had that night. Now, this is a relative issue obviously, given that a *New Yorker* cartoon often has some serious wisdom embedded in it, and it would be a gross exaggeration to say that all cartoons are frivolous or distracting. The cartoon in Carter's dream was full of meaning if one dug beneath its depths thoroughly. Ironically, a cartoon that presents itself in an exclusively visual montage that seems to *appeal* for a caption to *explain* its cryptic meaning is not unlike the structure of dream itself, whose manifest display has regressed almost totally from the verbal to the visual and awaits free-associative interpretive process to clothe it in words again.

Rodrigo (the Roderigo of *Othello* disguised slightly) seemed to be a representation of the ego ("Rodr" and "igo"—"ego") that processes reality sensibly and forthrightly, whereas the aggressive group that insists clients should be kept uninformed seemed to represent defensive strategies such as denial, disavowal, repression. The cave with its access to escape from torrential engulfing affects—murderous aggression, incestuous disregard for boundaries—suggested yet another line of defense: phobic flight and invocation of the miraculous. When I asked Carter why the "e" had been dropped from Roderigo, he answered after a pause: "Perhaps it's $e = mc^2$, energy and agency being disavowed." A paraphrase of his understanding of the dream could be summarized as follows: "I'm on the floor with my dysfunctional father 'mopping and moping.' The women have agency, my sarcastic comment about 'interactional' notwithstanding. I assign agency to the women and lowered status to the men even if I try to reclaim some agency with my 'interactional' comment. Roderigo with an 'e' (Iago's sidekick) represents my wish to overthrow Othello, who despite his innocent, gullible nature still represents not only my evil mother but also my weak father." Carter was expressing pre-oedipal and oedipal fury at both parents for the soul murder inflicted upon him for so many years. The cartoon represents all this in a mock-serious, even comic manner, as if a witty caption could be tagged onto this visual tableau and then one

160

could move on without considering the overdeterminations that are being disregarded. The caption could be thought of as a too-facile interpretation that illuminates momentarily by excluding the many other interpretations that also deserve consideration.

The original meaning of "cartoon" is derived from the Italian "cartone," which was a rather thick paper that afforded the old masters a hard surface to test out their drawings or sketchings on. (The more modern meaning of "cartoon" as "comedy" or "caricature" dates from the nineteenth century, when cartoons first began to appear in *Punch*.) If one considers the dream-work as an old master, could one argue that manifest content is the first preliminary sketch of the metamorphosis of latent dream thoughts into disguised visual representations that primary processes have condensed and displaced so drastically in the service of disguise? The manifest visual sketch does have to gain the approval of the censor if the visual cinematics are to get permission to continue. Surely there are situations in which the first manifest sketch is not disguised enough and is about to arouse the censor's disapproval. At such a moment might a cartoon that almost mocks the concept of visual representability entirely be just the device to fool the censor with its enigmatic flamboyance and captionless status until some clever caption explains the manifest visual scene acceptably? In that sense the cartoon is not the preliminary sketch but a much later montage that is designed specifically with disguise as its sole purpose. "Look at this," the dream-work seems to suggest. "Forget about the original visuals that were too transparent. And forget about those other dreams and their too-obvious meanings. Devote all your energy to this cartoon and your search for a caption to unriddle its enigma."

Just as a clever joke in a dream, as we have seen in chapter nine, has the function of distracting the dreamer from much-less-humorous content in the dream thoughts, so too a highly visual cartoon and its conviction that Rodrigo is a world-renowned economist is designed to steer the mind away from Iago's and Roderigo's murderous intent to destroy Othello (mother, father). Roderigo in that sense is the child whose soul has been murdered and who will not be satisfied until Othello (mother, father) have been totally destroyed. The four dreams taken as a whole dynamic statement of one night's psychology could be summarized:

> I was expecting a normal loving mother who would cherish me rather than the monster that reared me in actuality. I can pretend to mop floors with my defeated father, but I will attack the women who have reduced their men to that status. In a cartoon I can disguise my murderous intent by focusing attention on a renowned economist. I will pretend to submit to the greenhouse effect of my mother's contempt for the ecological development of the little endangered planet of my existence, but secretly I will plot her overthrow as surely as Iago and Roderigo brought down the almighty Othello. When my oceanic affects reach high tide, I will sweep all away with the sheer elemental power of my well-analyzed ego. All disavowed "e" for psychic energy will be restored to me.

Carter had one other association to the "green" in Professor Greenhouse. Was he not merely a "green," immature child when his soul was murdered, and was it not the greenhouse of psychoanalysis that had allowed his battered, wintered soul to regenerate itself in the *interactional* psychological nourishment of a healing relationship? If plants can grow even in winter in the right environment, can human minds not recover their capacity to grow also in the healing ambience of psychoanalysis, one daring free association after another?

12

A POEM AND A DREAM

A psychoanalyst does not turn to dreams primarily to extract from them their esthetic properties. He studies the manifest appearance of dreams and, with the dreamer's collaboration, arrives at latent meaning through the portals that free-associative keys have opened. This does not mean that an analyst or any other dream watcher is unaware of or lacks interest in the esthetic enchantment that many dreams create with their most artistic manifest images. An analyst is not unaware that dream experience may have been the first inkling of an artistic, uncanny, internal, and surreal life that nourished our ancestors before *art*, as we have come to know it, had any human provenance or cultural meaning whatsoever.

Was *dream* the first unconscious artistic statement that bent reality out of all recognition (even though past and current realities were the dream's raw material and days' residue, day after atavistic day), since the dawn of perception? In other words, before *Homo sapiens* had museums or pen and parchment, and art as a concept must have been far from the hunter's mind, were his dreams not strange internal images that may have begun to pave psychological roads toward philosophy, religion, poetry, and art—even before these concepts had any of their modern meanings? Was it dreams that made an artist of primal man, his dreams a kind of internal Lascaux that prefigured the numinous animals that would eventually find their esthetic permanence in ancient stone?

Ancient stone and modern parchment are separated by little esthetic time, it would seem. In fact, James Joyce was so fascinated by the esthetic properties of the dream that, after *Ulysses* (1922) had exhausted all narrative possibilities and frontiers (at least for him!), he planned to write his ultimate masterpiece (*Finnegans Wake* [1939]) using the dream as model (Ellmann, 1982). And William Butler Yeats claimed that his poem "The Cap and Bells" (1899) was nothing more than a dream that he wrote down exactly as it had appeared to him upon awakening. No doubt Yeats and Joyce introduced their own artistry into their final esthetic products, regardless of these disclaimers, with dream imagery informing their efforts rather than replacing them. My point here is that esthetic issues are not the cardinal concern of an analyst as a dream is being interpreted.

The manifest appearance of a poem, by contrast with the manifest appearance of a dream, is not thought of as a facade that conceals the real meaning of the poem. The poem contains depths that can only be arrived at after several readings (with Empson, [1966] even claiming that some of a poem's esthetic ambiguities can perhaps never be fathomed completely), and the actual sequence of words on the page represents the manifest artistry of the poet; no other words are ever available to the reader to lighten the burden of interpretation. What you see is what you get. Robert Frost's comment that "poetry is what is lost in translation" (Untermeyer, 1964, p. 18) hits this esthetic nail on the head and is often quoted in and out of context for that very reason.

If a poet were to supply all of his free-associative ruminations to one of his poems, this would be an extraordinary complementary document, to be sure, but it would not change the word order on the page, and it would not necessarily explain why a very particular word order creates an esthetic sensation that no other sequence of words could accomplish.

164

When Shakespeare (1606), in a throwaway line in *Antony and Cleopatra*, had a minor character, Lepidus, say, "Let all the number of the stars give light/To thy fair way!" (III.2.80–81), who can say why "all the number of the stars" has an esthetic impact, while "countless stars" or "innumerable stars" would leave the reader cold?

What appears to be a simple esthetic question such as this is actually terribly complex, and therefore applied analysis is confronted by an almost impossible task. Shengold (2004) emphasized the "alas" in Freud's (1928) oft-quoted, militaristic-sounding statement, "Before the problem of the creative artist, analysis must, alas, lay down its arms" (p. 177), thereby bringing attention to the esthetic longing of the analyst and his inevitable defeat, perhaps, in the mysterious playing fields or battlegrounds of art and art criticism. And Grubrich-Simitis (1996) commented on applied analysis in a challenging way:

> It must be conceded…that psychoanalysis of whatever school has difficulty in accounting for the formal constitutive aspects of both artistic and scientific creativity. The charges once brought by Flaubert against Sainte Beuve and Taine as critics can equally well be leveled at not a few psychoanalytic studies of Art: "that they don't take sufficient account of Art, of the work itself, of its construction, of its style, in short of everything that constitutes beauty" (p. 78).

I am not sure that psychoanalysis can account for these formal constitutive properties of beauty that Flaubert and Grubrich-Simitis bring to our attention. I am also not sure, however, that psychoanalysis can or should "lay down its arms," given how intriguing the topic is, and I must confess that an "alas" of my own was recently stimulated by a serendipitous analytic event.

165

A writer in analysis related a dream and a poem almost in one breath, the one clearly stimulated by the other, with only a few short hours of temporal space between them. I will present the analysand's dream and the poem, a brief description of the analysis of the dreamer, a thorough report of his associations to poem and dream, and then attempt to discuss what, if any, esthetic conclusions can be drawn from all this.

The Dream

The analysand related the following:

> In my dream, I awaken to find my house full of guests. I am surprised but ask if anyone would like air-conditioning. I look out the window and am alarmed to see so many people. There are stalls and tents, a circus atmosphere. I scream at my wife to explain the crowds of intruders. She answers, "Don Mattingly died in Florida," but I cannot hear her. I scream again that I cannot hear her. And again she says, "Don Mattingly died in Florida."

The Poem

> "Forked Animal"
> Hiding out in the open
> I shield my heart from the rain,
> The wind my only clothing,
> Is my name Abel or Cain?
> Time will never tell me.
> Memory leaves me cold.

Night and Day stand witness
As young blood turns to old.
Hiding out in the open
I shield my heart from the pain,
Bloodless stars above me,
My loss, the Pleiades' gain.

A Brief Description of the Analysis

The dreamer—let us call him Dimitri—is a journalist who has written essays, short stories, and poetry all his life, as well as, of course, his news articles from around the world, which have "kept bread on the table," as he would say with characteristic modesty. He would be reluctant to call himself a poet, even though the poem just cited I believe, qualifies as a fine piece of verse. It may not be canonical, but it is arresting and well crafted. It is brief, but deep and rather haunting in its simplicity.

Dimitri is seventy-six years old, married, with grown children and grandchildren. He was born in Latvia but has lived in New York since 1950. He has an older brother who still lives "in the old country," but the siblings never communicate. What began as sibling rivalry turned into a malicious adult hatred, which probably had a psychotic component as the older brother's envy of the younger's success and talent became delusional. This broke Dimitri's heart when he was young. Age has seasoned the wound, but a scar remains, which has found a reflection in this poem.

Dimitri's father was addicted to gambling and alcohol, losing most of his possessions (a farm, a small business) as his reckless life began to spin out of control. He was charming and childlike, and Dimitri's anger at him was as profound as it was repressed, never tapped until analysis was well under way. It seemed like a betrayal to be angry at such a tragic man, as

167

Dimitri's deep masochistic character traits suggest, and these traits are also reflected in the poem.

Dimitri's mother was the abiding stable relationship throughout his childhood. Her humor, her ebullience in the face of great personal hardship became his ideal, and he believed that some of his poetry was influenced by her, even though she had no intellectual aspirations whatsoever and never wrote a line of poetry in her life as far as Dimitri knew. But he remembered the rain in Latvia and her poetic depiction of it as coming from "an opening in the sky." To awaken him in the morning, she would scream with robust humor, "Wake up, Dimitri, wake up! You'll be dead long enough!" He loved the totality of her—even including the death wishes aimed at him! In analyzing dream and poem, he would become even more aware of how deeply she had insinuated herself—with his unwitting complicity, of course—into the very fabric of his poetry and his life.

I want to keep this biographical sketch to a minimum and concentrate entirely on what applied psychoanalysis can or cannot contribute to an understanding of the esthetic strategies that Dimitri's poem uses to capture the attention of its audience. The rest of this paper will address the poem and the dream and whether an understanding of the one can assist us in our deliberation on the other.

The poem and the dream, placed side by side, may not seem to be unconscious bedfellows or to bear much resemblance to each other at all, for that matter. The dream occurred not long after the analysand had been awakened briefly by dawn at his window. The dawn seemed Shakespearean to the dreamer, "in russet mantle clad," walking "o'er the dew of yon high eastern hill" (Shakespeare 1600–1601, I.1.166–167), and he awakened his wife to share the beauty with her. On returning to bed after this brief interval, he chuckled to his wife: "When you've seen one of these, you've seen them all!" Not to be outdone by this defensive, dawn-bashing cynic, his wife slyly counterpunched: "Dawn—she's too young for you anyway,

Dimitri. You're wise not to be too beguiled by her." On relating this to me, Dimitri remembered being proud of his wife's quick-witted repartee, and then falling back to sleep and dreaming the above-described dream.

When Dimitri awakened from the dream, a line of poetry came to him suddenly—"like an inspiration," it seemed—as if unbidden by any act of will but simply emerging from the unconscious. The line was "hiding out in the open" and seemed initially to be a reference to Dimitri's father, whom he thought of as lonely, tragic, and Lear-like. The dream had spawned this particular line, Dimitri felt, but how the gestation got started was a mystery. Within an hour, eleven more lines that seemed like associations to the dream imagery had appeared. Dimitri gave the poem the title "Forked Animal" because the atmosphere seemed so Lear-like to him. Dimitri had gone from a Shakespearean dawn to a Shakespearean blasted heath in an instant, it seemed, and the uncanny transformation would become clear only after a considerable amount of analytic process and deliberation.

Several weeks of analytic work made it possible to define the latent dream thoughts that Dimitri believed not only informed the manifest content of the dream, but also the "manifest content" of the poem. Dimitri believed that the "primal scene" of the dawn at his window (as he called it, only half-humorously) was the day's residue that got the unconscious engines started. As described earlier, the dawn seemed so unusually beautiful that he had awakened his wife to share the beauty with her. They both gazed at it, transfixed by first light and its esthetic artistry. "When you've seen one of these, you've seen them all," Dimitri commented—a defensive statement, a piece of humorous self-mockery whose full meaning became clear to him only after considerable free-associative rumination.

Initially, Dimitri's wife had teased him about his automatic, almost reflexive defensiveness, and it was in a humorous, if ironic, mood that he fell asleep again and dreamed the dream we have been addressing. As Dimitri began to "play" with the meaning of the dream and the subsequent poetic

169

creation, his defensiveness was better understood as he doggedly insisted on pursuing the latent thoughts that sparked and shaped both products. In the interest of parsimony and clarity of argument, the latent dream thoughts can be presented here "whole cloth" rather than as a series of free associations that stitched the fabric together over time.

Dimitri's initial humor about a primal scene led eventually to a more serious consideration of infantile sexuality and imagination. The beauty of an "innocent," youthful dawn peered at by Dimitri and his wife did seem like a reversal of childhood's arrangement, when infantile sexuality loses its innocence as curiosity takes the parental bedroom and its activities as location and subject matter for intense inquiry. His mother's directive to "wake up, Dimitri, you'll be dead long enough" and her description of rain as being produced "when the sky opens" seemed indicative of an ambivalent intimacy with her that Dimitri, as the transference neurosis unfolded, had come to think of as "primal." The relative lack of a substantial relationship with his father gave an intense oedipal cast to his early years; when peering through the window of childhood imagination at his parents' sexual life, he seemed to see a powerful woman and a diminished man, the woman capable of opening the sky or closing the eyes of the dead, while the man seemed to be a nonplayer in this poetic, dramatic but Gothic depiction of the world.

With this preamble as guide, we can enter into the world of Dimitri's dream thoughts, which I summarize as follows:

I see the flesh of the ever-youthful dawn (my mother) at my window. Night (my father) has been vanquished by the sexual power of first light. I am giddy with excitement as I imagine the seduction of the eternal mother and the total exclusion of her husband (my father).

The starkness of these thoughts was changed utterly by the dream-work, since the unconscious sense of guilt they aroused threatened to alert the censor and condemn all further dream construction outright. The defensive process that started so quickly, even while Dimitri was briefly awake prior to the dream construction (evidenced by the dismissal of dawn's uniqueness with the comment that "when you've seen one of these, you've seen them all") carried over into the dream and changed the latent thoughts drastically from a scene of seduction to a scene of deprivation and destruction, whereby Dimitri's house was overrun by strangers and his wife was announcing the death of Don Mattingly in Florida.

Dimitri was thrilled when he noticed the pun embedded in his wife's statement in the dream: wasn't "Don Mattingly" a clever translation of "Dawn Matinly" (the word "dawn" as noun and adverb, side by side) into the real-life Yankees slugger Don Mattingly, who was being pronounced dead! The dream-work is impressive and masterful as it translates every iota of sexuality and seduction into paranoia (a quiet house is transformed into a circus), while simultaneously expressing a reaction formation (the unwelcome guests are being offered air-conditioning!) and displaced death wishes (dawn and sexuality have been transformed into death and castration).

Since the aesthetics of *poem work* are even more centrally my topic here than the aesthetics of dream-work, the poem's manipulation of the dream thoughts will be focused on in what follows.

If we place the latent dream thoughts and the poem side by side, the transformation wrought by the poem work does seem as radical as the dream-work's distortions. Dream-work, however, with no audience in mind other than the dream censor it wishes to deceive with cunning disguises, can alter the latent dream thoughts drastically and with a total disregard for any communicative accountability. Poem work, as we have seen, can be drastic also, but some communicative continuity with a current

171

audience and some sense of competitive communicative continuity with all previous audiences and poets (what Harold Bloom [1973] has called the "anxiety of influence") must be maintained consciously, pre-consciously, or unconsciously.

In this case, I have argued that the poet has almost completely disguised the impulses and latent thoughts that got the dream and poem started. Is it possible that the poem is even more disguised than the dream? Since the poem "goes public" in the sense that it is written with an audience in mind, is disguise even more necessary? Does poem work have to work even harder than dream-work to conceal its latent meanings? But if the poet's open-minded mission is to reveal the hidden secrets of life to his presumably less open-minded, relatively repressed public, why would poem work have to conceal at all? Wouldn't full disclosure of all the mind's contents be the goal?

These questions, on reflection, make it clear that art is not at all about full disclosure. Like transference (or all aspects of psychoanalytic process, perhaps), it reveals and disguises all at once. Transference, as Freud taught us, tries to pin something on the analyst that there is an initial unwillingness to recognize in the self. This is the only mirror the self can use to recognize itself, eventually: it is as if self-deception is the only means available to arrive at eventual self-knowledge, if one is willing to go through the laborious transferential hall of mirrors that psychoanalytic process represents.

Is art not a similar hall of mirrors, perhaps, in which the artist attempts to reveal the hidden recesses of meaning while keeping a lot of his private self to himself? "In every work of art, chaos must shimmer through the regular veil of order," as Novalis put it, capturing the dichotomous conflict of the artist in one elegant sentence (O'Brien, 1995, p. 312).

The irony of revelation and disguise that poetry represents is captured in the first five words of Dimitri's poem, which announce boldly that exposure is the great tragic topic that the poem will take up—and yet we have come to realize that a whole other topic is being concealed. At first Dimitri had the uncanny conviction that the first line of his poem encapsulated his father's tragic existence and strange psychological nature with a brevity that was staggering. How could a man's life and complexity be so summed up in five words! As the free-associative wheels continued to turn, however, Dimitri came to see that the line "hiding out in the open" and an earlier one, "I shield my heart from the rain," were also striking defensive allusions to his mother and her comments about sky and rain and openings. In this context, "I shield my heart from the rain" had a pun in it (hiding out in the open, so to speak) that Dimitri seemed not to notice until the analyst hinted at it.

As mentioned earlier, Dimitri uncovered the pun "Don Mattingly"/"Dawn Matinly" early in his free associations to the dream, marveling at the unconscious artistry behind such transformations. In fact, his stumbling on this hidden pun in his associations became the key that unlocked the entire defensive strategy of the dream. But the poem also had a pun in it, which Dimitri had missed at first. The word "rain" concealed "reign" and "rein" and the French "reine" (queen), suggesting that if rain held an obvious allusion to his mother, the oedipal *reins* that could guide Dimitri's horse toward the conquest (*reign*) of his queen (*reine*) were too conflicted to handle!

In time, Dimitri would reflect on the ease with which the dream pun revealed its secret to him, whereas the poem's pun on rain seemed repressed and unavailable. If Dimitri was identified with his father's lonely existential isolation, he seemed equally identified with his mother, even if he wished to shield his heart from her. In the first two lines of the poem, has he not done precisely what the dream-work has done: he has changed seductive, sexual thoughts into hiding and shielding, with instinct masquerading as defense quicker than one can say "forked animal"! If *forked animal* is a reference to Lear, it is the bifurcated, conflictual nature of a dreaming, poetic animal that is being emphasized.

"The wind my only clothing" is a line of great existential anguish that ushers in the haunting question "Is my name Abel or Cain?" In other words, the first stanza depicts a Lear-like man—stark-naked (the wind his only clothing) and unsure if he is killer or victim. Isn't this the primal lover at the window, ogling the sexual dawn, but totally disguised as the furtive, castrated hero in hiding?

The ever-youthful, sexual dawn/mother at the window seems to have been banished completely. She may be hiding out in the open, but she is difficult to see, since she seems to have had a gender change and has become a Lear-like, naked, forked animal, clothed only by the wind, shielding her heart from the rain. To be sure, the gender of the poem's narrator is disclosed only by line four's question, "Is my name Abel or Cain?"—but this revelation throws the reader off the "scent of the woman" that got the poem started! The introduction of the Abel/Cain theme further disguises the sexuality of the latent dream/poem thoughts, even though it obviously accentuates the oedipal "total exclusion" of the father/brother theme as "night (my father) has been vanquished by the sexual power of first light." The Abel/Cain question introduces the idea of oedipal guilt (displaced onto the biblical sibling issue, to be sure), and the confusion at the heart of the question is left unresolved, just as the question itself is never answered.

A similar introduction of a sibling theme was used by Coleridge in a much longer poem, "The Rime of the Ancient Mariner," in which the guilty mariner is eventually saved in the "Pilot's Boy" episode. It has been argued (Mahon, 1987) that this is a reference to a genetic event in Coleridge's childhood, an intense sibling conflict with his brother Frank, which "sneaked" into the great poem's finale with an unconscious urgency that seemed unstoppable, regardless of any esthetic, last-minute awkwardness it may have dragged along with it in its unconscious wake!

Returning to Dimitri's much shorter poem, we are aiming to focus exclusively on the poem work and the nature and function of its disguises. The second stanza suggests that time, memory, and experience witness the guilt and suffering of the forked animal but do nothing about it. This is more Beckett than Freud, perhaps; but, again, it emphasizes the harshness of reality—its rind rather than the juicy, sexual, appetizing, fruity pulp of its interior. The latent thoughts of sexual triumph have been replaced by starkness, pain, suffering, loneliness, and guilt. This is Oedipus at Colonus, not the cocky young Oedipus who is about to approach the fated crossroads at Thebes. The third stanza suggests that the only winners in this dark depiction of the human condition (or in the Oedipus complex) are the Pleiades—nature herself, in other words, who lures mortal man to the window of desire day after day with a new and ancient dawning of unconscious yearning, which seems to offer eternal satisfaction but in the final analysis disappoints the foolish, oedipal, forked animal.

In this kind of cosmic Darwinism, human loss equals gain for the Pleiades, the seven daughters of Atlas and Pleione. They were pursued by Orion but rescued by Zeus, who turned them into doves and then placed them in the sky. Only six are visible as stars; one is perpetually in hiding. Six were loved by gods, and only Merope had to be content with the love of a mere mortal, Sisyphus—hence she shines less brightly in the sky than do her sisters. It was this more human, Sisyphean version of the mythological creature that Dimitri had unconsciously identified with, bending mythology to his own purposes, to be sure, and clearing a space for such revisionism in his poem. Thus, the poet seems to be surrendering his entropic molecules to the bloodless stars, dutifully paying his debt (and his death) to the exacting exigencies of nature. But, secretly, he identifies with the rebellious star that "hides out in the open"—waiting for dawn to appear, no doubt, as the orbit of sexual desire "dawns matinly," as long as flesh has the lure of instinct to guide it.

The poem work, by turning latent thoughts of seduction and sexual fulfillment into a *cri de coeur* of existential man at his most vulnerable, a guilty wretch with seemingly little interest in the *joie* of sexual ambitious life, seduces the reader in subtle, esthetic ways, and it is the nature of this strange seduction that will be addressed next. If the three stanzas of the poem are disguised verbal representatives of the dream thoughts, the disguise is practically complete. Dawn is never mentioned, and sexuality and a primal scene are not easy to intuit. However, as Dimitri's insights gradually coalesced, he became aware that the poem presses its nose at the window of the reader's house, so to speak, like a seductive dawn that insists on awakening the dreamer and the reader to its luminous charms. A spell is cast on the reader: he is being seduced to identify with the tragic, existential plight of a naked hero, a poor forked animal trapped in the finite axes of the human condition under a thoughtless sky. The raw materials of dream thoughts that were sexually explicit have been changed dramatically into existential wails that sound like the cries of a wounded animal but are quite seductive nevertheless.

In fact, one could argue that the formal constitutive elements of this esthetic sleight of hand are an elaborate disguise of explicit desire and a replacement of it with masochistic tragic imagery that seduces in its own way. The reader may not be conscious of the elaborate and disguised seduction, but, since the reader is a poor forked animal also, he will appreciate on some level how desire and defensive denials and transformations operate. He will, after all, have had experience with his own dreams and the complexity of their disguises.

How can a poet capture and seduce the reader, even though he may have changed his latent thoughts so drastically? Chukovsky (1925), in his advice to those attempting to write poetry for young children, suggests that he knows the answer to that question. In his thirteen commandments for writers of children's poetry, he suggests that, since young children are active creatures with shorter attention spans than those of adults, poems that seek to engage them must flit from image to image and must be full of rapid action to match this great fluidity of images in motion. Consequently, children love verbs, which are active, and they hate adjectives, which slow down the action. They love the dance of the troche. They love rhyme, and ideally the rhyming part of a poem carries the bulk of its meaning.

Chukovsky wrote about children from ages two to five. Things will change, obviously, as they grow older. And if Chukovsky knows how to capture the attention of children, how one captures and seduces the adult reader is another matter. Charles Lamb (1994) believed that he could distinguish Shakespeare's pen from Fletcher's in their collaborations, but recognition of Shakespeare's stylistic genius is not quite the same as defining its formal constitutive elements, a task that may forever elude the literary analyst (and applied analyst as well—alas). What we can say about Dimitri's poem is that it is seductive and that the reader identifies with the plight of the forked animal, recognizing a kinship with that component of the universal Oedipus complex that mourns with Oedipus at Colonus more readily, perhaps, than it embraces the hubris and sexually ambitious accomplishments of the pre-Colonus hero. With the phrase "hiding out in the open," Dimitri suggests (very indirectly and covertly, to be sure) that even a blind Oedipus can see the rich inner sexual life of the mind and body, as long as he refuses to ignore the body's charms and dreams and ambitions, no matter how inexorably and pitilessly "young blood turns to old."

Dimitri, who became defensive even as he was chanting the praises of the dawn to his wife (as evidenced by his comment that "when you've seen one of these, you've seen them all"), nevertheless managed to seduce the reader secondarily, even if the primary target of his sexuality and attention had to be ignored. The poem work turned a defensive maneuver into an esthetic one: by using rhyme, metaphor, mythology, and primary processes of displacement, condensation, and symbolism, in less than a hundred words, the poem seduces not directly but very *in*directly, as the reader identifies with Lear-like, universal affects that pull at human heartstrings, from Homer's time to Beckett's time, consciously and unconsciously. The simplicity of the singsong lines (suggesting a nursery rhyme or ballad) provides a jolting contrast to the Lear-like imagery that predominates. If this is the ballad of a forked animal, there is no hint of the balladeer romancing the dawn from his veranda! Dawn Matinly/Don Mattingly has certainly been wiped out of the poem almost entirely, as seductive dawn and powerful slugger are replaced by the furtive, guilty, and confused Abel/Cain character.

Those great primary processes of disguise that the dreamer can exploit with seemingly total disregard for coherence must be curbed and modified by the poet, at least in the manifest facade of his communication. The latent bulk of unconscious communication in poetry probably has as much access to the full range of primary processes as dreams do. The interweaving of the two likely defines the formal constitutive skills of the poet as he disguises unconscious raw material in manifest facade, but also allows chinks to appear in the esthetic armor, so that human vision can peer through and reveal to itself the seductive nakedness of raw unconscious yearning.

If defense and instinct form an alloy that a compromise called the human condition has exploited ever since it could be called human, neurosis—a creative compromise formation that is pretty universal itself—has a counterpart in art, which also transforms instinct into esthetic representations or misrepresentations of itself. Neurosis recognizes itself in art, art recognizes itself in neurosis, and it is this doppelgänger effect that pulls the reader into the esthetic illusion with almost the same intensity as instinct itself. Poem work, like dream-work, seduces the awakener/reader with one manifestation of itself that leads to deeper communion with less obvious latent manifestations of itself, if he dares to follow.

What poem work hides and reveals is at the heart of a great mystery called "aesthetics." The primary processes Freud discovered compress and conceal and distort, and the resultant intensity of that compression packs a wallop. Mannoni (1971) has suggested that Freud's joke book (1905) may have been his first attempt to crack the code of the esthetic mystery. I would like to suggest that a joke is a little coil of compressed meanings: it jolts the listener and releases pent-up (repressed) energies (the incentive bonus or bonus of pleasure, as Freud called it), which results in the immediate affective response of laughter. All art may possess equally condensed coils of compressed meaning that spring out at the reader like esthetic jack-in-the-boxes, not always inducing laughter, to be sure, but certainly releasing profound affects of empathy and understanding. The artist and his audience, the poet and his reader, approach this jack-in-the-box (or Russian box) of compressed meanings within meanings with precarious expectancy, like a face reading itself in a mirror at the first startling moment of perception and recognition. Baudelaire (1857) captured this startling duality when he addressed the reader with provocative irony: "Hypocrite lecteur,—mon semblable,—mon frère!" (p. 6).

If dream-work's compression of meaning into compact, primary-processed obfuscation is completely unconscious, poem work's artistry must represent a collaboration of conscious and unconscious components that make poetry accessible and intelligible on one level and mysterious and baffling on another. Any line of Dimitri's poem seems simple and straightforward on first reading, and yet there is an aftertaste that is disquieting and haunting.

Take "memory leaves me cold," for example. The expression "it leaves me cold" might be used as a comment about an artistic product that does not arouse the expectable emotional reaction; something abstract (like art) is being judged by the impact it has on the body: the *psychological* is being put to the *physiological* test, so to speak, to see whether it is the real thing, an artistic product that can grab you by the flesh and move you. "It leaves me cold" is a more powerful way of saying "it had no emotional impact on me." Words referring to the body and the elemental carry more clout than abstract or intellectual referents. An artistic product made by a fellow human being can be judged by whether it affects the body "on a gut level." The body temperature of a work of art can be assessed by its effect on the body of the audience, with "it leaves me cold" constituting a near-damning evaluation. "Memory leaves me cold" consequently expresses an idea that jolts, since memory, after all, is not an external artistic product that is being judged.

Memory is the *self* or a major component of it. Memory is man's great compensation for all that experience is powerless to hold on to. Man has the illusion of mastering the past by keeping a record of it. If repetition compulsion is a caricature in action of this most prized ego function, memory's internal function itself is one of nature's finest achievements. But it has limitations. It is finite and mortal, no matter how photographic or reliable it may seem. Dimitri's line reminds the reader of the fragility of the human mind and its products—that it is mortal porcelain they are made of, not immortal steel. Time (night and day) and memory witness the entropy of human flesh; they are powerless to do anything about it. Dimitri's frustration with the limitations of human memory is an indictment—not only of analysis that puts such stock in memory retrieval but also of the whole cultural and memorial enterprise of the human condition itself.

"Like a piece of ice on a hot stove," as Frost (1939) said, "the poem must ride on its own melting" (p. 778). Poetry and memory can record the entropic melting, but they are powerless to do anything about it. The irony is that Dimitri's poem, which might have been a serenade to the dawn rather than a song of entropy, ends up melting into its own form of beauty anyway.

One final clinical comment about the uniqueness of a poem in the psychoanalytic process: I would like to suggest that a poem in the context of clinical process may be different from a dream, with the latter never being off-limits to free-associative access, whereas a poem, once fixed in esthetic time and space, may resist or defy further analysis, given the analysand's reticence to tamper with a sublimation that seems final.

This raises interesting countertransference issues: after the poem "Forked Animal" seemed to have become unalterable as an esthetic entity, the analyst had a further association to the name "Mattingly" that had earlier eluded him. Wasn't there another hidden pun here on "mating" and "matting," the one sexual and the other a cover-up? Wasn't Dimitri's oedipal wish to "mate" with the ageless dawn quite the opposite of his wish to cover it up with "matting," and wasn't this yet another version of his defensive "when you've seen one of these, you've seen them all"?

Analytic tact suggested that the analyst should leave well enough alone and allow the sublimation to "defend" itself without further interpretive interference. "Mating" and "matin" and "matting" were not devoid of many alternative free-associative points of entry and had been pretty well explored already, and nothing seemed lost by leaving a few esthetic, if defensive, stones unturned.

Dimitri was a modest man who would have dismissed any attempt to read more into one hundred words or so than seemed warranted. With a similar modesty, I have offered a comparison between poem work and dream-work that may shed a little light on the mystery of beauty without attempting to at all codify the precise ingredients that make art what it undoubtedly is: a creative compromise of man, a forked esthetic animal in all his frailty and glory, hiding out in the open without a shred of immortal certainty to his name.

13
TRUMP DREAMS

A highly educated, liberal middle-aged man whose analysis was nearing termination was alarmed when he had a series of what he called "Trump Dreams." As a very brief sketch of his analysis and the genetic events most often worked on in the transferences of analytic process, it could be said that his father's lifelong passivity and depression had often led to bouts of passivity and depression in himself, such was the nature of his identification with the long-suffering parent. Modeling himself on a series of alternate "fathers" (both real and imagined) and gifted with considerable innate talents, he had become a remarkable success not only in business but also in his responsibilities as a devoted husband and father to his wife and children. When he regressed into passive states and dark moods, he would work hard in analysis to recover his agency as quickly as possible. He had come to learn in analysis that a mood reflected only a regressed facet of his character and not the whole entity.

The Trump Dreams, as he called them derisively at first, until he came to realize that derision was merely a defense, alarmed him for many reasons. His antipathy for Trump was deep and serious. He contributed generously to whatever political initiatives he believed might "topple the tyrant" as soon as possible. His initial disgust with himself for dreaming about Trump led to critical insights not only about politics in general but about the internal politics of dynamic conflicted intrapsychic unconscious life as well. He was pleased that he could "use the scoundrel to understand myself better," as he put it, having analyzed the dreams.

Here are the dreams as reported:

> A young man challenges what Trump is saying. The young man's name is Richardson, a business colleague of the analysand. "No, not Richardson—a younger person," a voice in the dream announces. Trump orders his henchmen to remove the challenger, justifying his action by saying, "I have only two weeks until the election." There is a huge tent. I want to leave. Wife says, "No, you should stay." Earlier in the dream I was supposed to play a part in Trump's production of *Richard III*. Trump goes to get his own copies of the play. He returns without them. He says he'll get a paperback copy in the adjacent bookstore. I can learn my lines if I have a copy.

Later that night the analysand dreams about Trump again.

> Trump appears again. Pianist comes out of concert hall. Trump says: "I told you piano was no good." I seem surprised that Trump knows anything about pianos. Scene changes: Interior of a building. Candide (a woman in the dream) nudges dreamer and another business colleague, saying, "We could take over," meaning the three of us.

In an even later dream that night, the analysand dreams a dream with the sparsest content:

> Trump was friendly.

And a fourth dream follows, not quite a Trump dream but political and in the same vein somewhat:

Paul Ryan with long hair. Looks poetic.

The analysand was puzzled by this profusion of "Trump Dreams," as he called them. But he got to work, associating freely in his usual systematic fashion. His first association went to *Richard III*. He knew many colleagues named Richard, most of them trusted friends. There was one, however, a business colleague who had "trumped" him once in a business deal by pretending to be in dire financial straits and thereby eliciting more "charitable" terms from the analysand in complex negotiations. When he learned years later that he had been trumped (deceived, outsmarted), an ambivalent attitude developed toward this business colleague. He still had close connections with this "Richard," whom he had never challenged about the deceptive business ploy, but he believed that unresolved antipathy toward this Richard was one of the overdetermined themes in the dream, as if he wished to play the part of Richard III and dispatch such villains with sadistic relish. That led to thoughts about Richardson, who challenged Trump in the dream until the dreamer seemed to disavow it, saying it was a younger person. This led to thoughts about a son, the son of Richard, rivalrous with his father. Since most of the Richards in his life were beloved, and only one Richard considered untrustworthy, the analysand believed he was "splitting" in the dream, dispatching the "bad" Richard while retaining the "good" others. This led to the deepest level of latent meaning: he knew that he resented his father's psychological and emotional collapse.

Throughout all the years of his early development, his father was a presence characterized by the emotional absence chronic depression entailed. Until he began analysis he had never been able to articulate how furious he was with his father's neglect of him. The idea that this beloved country must now endure the abuse of power that Trump represented resonated with the genetic abuse he had endured throughout his childhood as the father "abused" his power by total abdication of it. That he, a citizen of a country that had been "fathered" by Washington, Jefferson, Lincoln must now endure the ignominy of being "fathered" by Trump seemed like a cruel replay of what he had already endured in childhood and had vowed never to be subjected to again.

The dreams stirred up questions. Why were the dreams' manifest contents making Trump seem more intellectual, more aesthetically informed than Trump in reality is? His associations led to other disreputables who had held high office—Richard Nixon, Dick Cheney. He had read in the *Economist* an article about Cheney's artificial heart, which asserted that Dick Cheney, given that artificial hearts have continuous flow rather than human pulse rhythms, hadn't had a heartbeat for ten years! "As if he had one before that," the analysand said, chuckling with mischievous glee. Was Trump Richard III even if his name was Donald? A joke making the rounds of his office supplied a clue as to the association between Trump and Richard III. The joke references the three biggest Dicks of all time: tricky Dicky Nixon, heartless Dick Cheney, and Trump the biggest dick of all. So that humorous sequence would make Trump Richard III, the biggest Dick of all.

Over the next several days the analysand continued to free associate to the so-called Trump Dreams. Trying to connect manifest and latent content, the analysand played with the name Richardson in the first Trump dream. Richardson challenges Trump at first. This is then denied: it was not Richardson but a younger person. When Trump's henchmen remove Richardson by force, Trump justifies this by saying he has only two weeks left until the election. The analysand thought this was not only a reference to political thuggery but to transference and termination as well. The younger analysand (he was twenty or more years younger than the analyst), who was thinking of dismissing his analyst (removing the analyst from the seat of power) as he claimed the individuation analysis had fostered and promoted in him, had an oedipal urgency that seemed obvious to both parties of the analytic dyad. The two weeks to election seemed like an obvious reference to termination, not in two weeks, but on a mutually agreed upon schedule. Termination could feel like being removed hastily from analysis by the "henchman" analyst, or it could feel like a triumphant culmination of a piece of work well done, depending on the prevailing unconscious mood as the whole topic was under consideration from session to session.

The analysand was intrigued by the transformation of Trump not only into an impresario interested in putting on a performance of *Richard III* in the first dream but also into a concertgoer who knew something about pianos (in Dream 2), and even a friendly presence in Dream 3. These transformations seemed to be manifest frantic machinations of a latent dream-work that needed to alter the monster's appearance lest dream turn to nightmare and the whole disguise of sleeping and dreaming be unmasked too precipitously, oneiric illusion the casualty.

Dream 4, with Paul Ryan's metamorphosis into a long-haired poetic romantic type, seemed to betray the dream-work's similar insistence on drastic illusion as opposed to the brutality of monstrous reality. The analysand's most poignant association to all these drastic examples of unconscious defensive metamorphosis of harsh reality into an illusory opposite was his own childhood, in which a frighteningly dysfunctional father had to be transformed into a family romance of fairy tale alternate fathers (his uncle, his older sibling, inspirational teachers, his empathetic, insightful analyst, to name a few). The genetic and the transferential went hand in hand, of course, as time present and time past merge in such examples of analytic process.

The analysand was intrigued by the dream-work's guile in employing a parapraxis in Dream 1 that exposes Trump's masquerade so cunningly. (Mahon, 2005, cited parapraxes in dreams as unusual nested phenomena that have a most defensive nature and function.) Trump, promising to fetch a copy of *Richard III* so that the dreamer can learn his lines forgets to follow through on his promise and a paperback copy of *Richard III* from an adjacent bookstore must suffice "so that the dreamer can learn his lines." The dream-work's ambivalence seems palpable. The latent wish became obvious: "I wish Trump were not president, not really Richard III, but merely an impresario putting on a play about Shakespeare's intriguing villain." The genetic corollary is even more poignantly significant: "I wish my father were not a dysfunctional man whose passivities banished his children to a tower of deprivation and neglect not unlike Richard III's abuse of the doomed children in the Tower of London." The transference wish as termination was being considered could be paraphrased as: "I wish my analyst were not discharging me from analysis 'scarce half made up.'" The analysand knew that he was whole and not at all "scarce half made up," but there was great ambivalence about ending a relationship that had meant so much to him. There was great anger at the analyst for agreeing with him that he was ready to leave as opposed to insisting on an interminable analysis in which the loving analyst would replace the dysfunctional father permanently. I have entitled this brief communication "Trump Dreams," but it could as readily be called "Termination Dreams," given that it was reflections on termination and not merely on politics that had triggered them.

The appearance of Candide in Dream 2 led to many fruitful associations. Candide's suggestion that "we can take over" seemed like an oedipal triumph in which analysand and mother take over since father is "out of it." The friendly Trump in Dream 3 would seem to be father's friendly acceptance of the hostile oedipal takeover by Candide and the analysand. The word "Candide" was ripe for associative exploration in and of itself.

"Candide" could be broken into "Can" and "Deed." At the core of the analysand's neurosis was the conviction that his unconscious "deeds" had indeed magically killed the father and rendered him dysfunctional for the rest of his life. "Can," on the other hand, seemed to hold a more adaptive promise in the sense that in fantasy a man *can* kill his father metaphorically if the father is healthy enough to be able to tolerate—not only tolerate but relish—this enactment in fantasy. Surely it is this metaphorical understanding of the Oedipus complex, its potential in fantasy (the "can" of it as opposed to the actual deed of it) that makes adaptive resolution possible.

The analysand spent time on the whole topic of learning one's lines. A fiercely independent-minded and original thinker, he criticized analysis as a place where you go to learn your lines, all too often the analyst's lines. This was transference, of course, from a childhood in which he had to subdue his own fury at a passive father and a school atmosphere that at its worst seemed like learning the lines dictated by authoritarian elders rather than a cultivation of one's own lines, one's own innate creativities and unique points of view. But it was also transference as seen through the lens of termination. The analysand was very much aware that his wish to learn the analyst's lines was a defense against the wish to send the analyst to hell and completely individuate by insisting on his own script entirely. To become a mere learner of lines seemed like education derailed to him, or analysis derailed if one could only experience the thrill of the analytic situation as a mere slavish imitation of the master/analyst's spoon-fed interpretations. The analysand was very much aware that he had imbibed his father's pathological passivities into his own unconscious mind as a child through processes of identification out of a perverse kind of loyalty to parental ineptitude. He had learned his father's lines but not his own, so to speak. He did not want to repeat that tragedy as his analysis came to a close. He often saw childhood as the mold and analysis as the breaker of molds of predestination: by insisting on exposing seductive pathological misguided loyalties to early genetic traumatic events, analysis insists on exchanging magical thinking for the adaptive logic of reality. Toward the end of his analysis, this issue had been examined enough, he believed. He could learn so much from his analyst without compromising his own voice, his own individuality at all. On the one hand, the analysand, like Richard III, feels dispatched by the analyst into the unknowns of a new sense of individuation "scarce half made up." On the other hand, the analysand feels that he has de-idealized the analyst and can therefore terminate with a sense of power in his own equality in this best of all possible post-analytic worlds. (Another Panglossian reference to Candide perhaps?)

One of my aims in this brief communication has been to suggest that the Trump Dreams were not just political statements, since all dreams are much more than the razzle-dazzle of manifest content. Analysis has cultural, social, and political aspects, to be sure, as well as a most private one. Political activism is a triumph over the kind of passivity demagogues seek to instill in an intimidated citizenry. Analytic activism is a triumph over the "mind-forged" (Blake, 1794) learned passivities of neurosis, as manifested most glaringly in transferential process. There was no conflict between them as they sought to expose the twin tyrannies of political fascism as parodied in dreams and psychological fascism that slavishly learns the lines of an unconscious intrapsychic tyranny called neurosis.

In one of his last interviews, Philip Roth, when asked, "Does Donald Trump outstrip the novelist's imagination?" answered: "It isn't Trump as a character, a human type—the real estate type, the callow and callous killer capitalist—that outstrips the imagination. It is Trump as president of the United States." Perhaps Roth is partially wrong and perhaps it is possible that dream—an esthetic human product, as suggested in this brief communication—has the power to take the measure of political monsters and put them to work in the service of psychoanalysis.

14

JAMES JOYCE AND THE DREAM:
A PSYCHOANALYTIC INQUIRY

Introduction

James Joyce was fascinated with dreams and the dreaming process. For years he interpreted his own dreams and the dreams of his wife and others. He was fascinated not only by the actual content of dreams and approaches to interpreting them, but he was also interested in what he called "the esthetic of the dream," which he used in the most extraordinary manner in the composition of *Finnegans Wake*. It is not easy to know precisely what Joyce meant by the "esthetic of the dream," but he does seem to be suggesting that a dream, like a work of art, must get created by some mysterious artistic process. Invoking the "muse" to explain the god-like birth of the artist's creation does not really clarify the mystery; Freud's intuition of primary processes gets closer to the core of the mystery, at least in relation to the structure of a dream. Are there primary artistic processes that engineer the structure of a work of art? Freud seemed disheartened that he could never discover them. "Before the genius of the creative artist, psychoanalysis must alas lay down its arms," Freud says, his "alas" in this military metaphor betraying an emotion of defeat, perhaps (Shengold, 2004). Silvano Arieti (1976) in his *Creativity: The Magic Synthesis* suggests that in creativity the primary processes and the secondary processes join forces to give birth to tertiary processes that orchestrate the wonder that is art.

Joyce's methodology in *Finnegans Wake* was an attempt to write a novel of puns and primary process neologisms as if the novel were written by a Joycean dream-work rather than by the creative ego of the novelist himself. Obviously, the novel *was* written by Joyce's waking genius, which created the illusion of the language of dream rather than the language of waking life. He called *Ulysses* his day book and *Finnegans Wake* his night book. If *Ulysses* revolutionized the novel with its stream-of-consciousness style, as if it were a free-associative text from start to finish, *Finnegans Wake*, which Joyce spent seventeen years of his life perfecting, using the esthetic of dream, as he called it, to guide him, is as baffling as the manifest content of the most perplexing dreams. If Joyce has indeed identified with the dream-work, he has certainly come up with one of the most mysterious dreams ever recorded.

As a developing writer Joyce considered pursuing poetry, but when he realized that he could not compete with Yeats, he turned to prose exclusively. That said, his poems in *Pomes Penyeach* are very accomplished: the poem "She Weeps Over Rahoon" is pure music and indeed has been put to music by several American composers, including Miriam Gideon. And, of course, the last paragraph of "The Dead," though written as prose, is truly the most moving poetry in and of itself. Looking at the volume of his prose output, the sequential development of each achievement is impressive. *A Portrait of the Artist as a Young Man* depicts his childhood and early years; and in *Dubliners*, written in a prose style as accomplished as Flaubert's, he tries to depict what he thought of as the "paralysis" of his native city. But *Ulyssses* is written in a revolutionary manner, as if he had become acquainted with the concept of free associations, which he now transformed into a verbal stream-of-consciousness technique that changed the novel utterly and became, with Eliot's *The Waste Land*, an early iteration of modernism. In *Finnegans Wake* (known only as Work in Progress for the seventeen years he spent laboring over this last literary product, as it would turn out to be, Joyce dying in 1941 at the age of fifty-eight) he would address the greatest challenge of his literary career: he would write a novel using *the esthetic of the dream!* And indeed, as mentioned earlier, *Finnegans Wake* reads like the manifest content of a very lengthy dream! It could be argued that Joyce used two psychoanalytic principles to great effect: he used free-associative principles to write *Ulysses* and then turned to dream-work and dream construction to create his most challenging novel, *Finnegans Wake*, using the esthetic of the dream..

The Esthetic of Dream

Joyce described what he meant by the esthetic of the dream to Eugene Jolas:

Joyce felt an affinity with Freud, citing the similarity in their names: he was referring to the "joy" in Joyce and the "freude" (joy) in Freud. It was a negative affinity, however, since as he remarked derisively once on being questioned about psychology, "Psychology! What can a man know but what passes through his mind?" Joyce was clearly asserting that the creative mind was a flow of spontaneities that could never be assembled into an organized categorical system. Whereas Freud would find evidence of unconscious agency in parapraxes (slips of the tongue, et cetera), Joyce would proclaim through the mouth of Stephen Dedalus in *Ulysses* that "the man of genius makes no mistakes. His errors are volitional and are the portals of creativity." It is not clear whether Joyce had read *Die Traumdeutung* (*The Interpretation of Dreams* by Freud), but one can assume that he had, given his voracious literary appetite. (From Ellmann's book *Ulysses on the Liffey*, we learn that in his library in Paris and in Trieste, Joyce had copies of *Leonardo da Vinci, A Memory of His Childhood* and *The Psychopathology of Everyday Life*, both in German).

That said, Joyce's method of dream interpretation seems entirely idiosyncratic and intuitive. Still, his friends seemed amazed at his analytic confidence and told him their dreams as if approaching an oracle. Ellmann asserts, however, that "Joyce's interpretations showed the influence of Freud," despite his disdain for the Freudian method. Despite this disdain, Joyce kept a dream book in 1916 "in which he noted down Nora's dreams with his own interpretations" (Ellmann, p. 436). I would like to present Joyce's interpretations of dreams, especially his wife's and two of his own, including his insightful thoughts and questions about his friends' dreams, always keeping in mind, of course, that he was primarily interested in how he could use the *strangeness* of dream content to fashion a revolutionary novel. But I must begin on a biographical note to flesh out the genetics that spawned not only his development but what he used to transform reality into the alchemy of artistic creation.

Joyce: Biography as the Fount of His Creativity

We know that Joyce had three brothers: Stanislaus, two years younger than James, born December 17, 1884; Charles Patrick, born July 24, 1886, and George Alfred, born July 4, 1887. There were also six female siblings,(Eileen, Eva May, Mabel, Margaret Alice, Florence, and May Kathleen) and of course, James himself, born February 2, 1882, was the eldest of the surviving children; the firstborn, a boy, had lived only a few days. We do not know what effect the death of his predecessor sibling had on James Joyce, but we can assume he was born into a climate of grieving parents and that the shadow of the dead boy fell across his childhood for quite some time. John Joyce's lament over the death in 1881 of his firstborn son was expressed in bitter words: "My life was buried with him." Little wonder that a child's coffin would appear in James Joyce's dreams many years later, memory being the inconsolable, guilty thing that it is. In one of his letters Joyce says, "Absence is the highest form of presence," and anyone who has experienced grief knows how uncanny grief revenants can be.

Joyce uses his family, transformed, for whatever esthetic effect he was seeking, throughout his writings. As Mary T. Reynolds writes: "He transforms the family in numbers, in relationships, and in the personal characteristics of individual members." In "Joyce and His Brothers: The Process of Fictional Transformation," Reynolds writes that the transformation of the four Joyce brothers in the three novels, *Stephen Hero*, *A Portrait of the Artist as a Young Man*, and *Ulysses* are most interesting. Joyce's youngest brother, George, died in March 1902, when Joyce was twenty years old and in his last year of college. In *Stephen Hero* (an early draft of *A Portrait of the Artist as a Young Man*) George appears not as himself but as the dying Isabel. In August 1903, Joyce's mother died, suggesting that the fictional death of Isabel in *Stephen Hero* is a composite of two deaths that shook Joyce deeply. He wrote this chapter of *Stephen Hero* in 1905, the year that his first child was born, named George after his dead brother.

The short story "Eveline" in *Dubliners* seems to be based on Joyce's eldest sister, Margaret Alice, also known as Poppie. (Incidentally, John Joyce was called Pappie by his children.) After the death of her mother, Poppie postponed her wish to go to a convent and vowed to take care of the children as her mother would have. When Stanislaus and James sent money home from the Continent, Pappie would intercept it and drink half the amount before it ever got to Poppie to use for childcare. The short story tells of Eveline's wish to go with Frank, her lover, to Buenos Ayres, but at the last minute, as the boat is ready to sail and Frank is exhorting her to hurry onto the boat with him, she cannot leave. This is a most complex image of the unconscious struggle Nora Barnacle and Joyce must have felt as they abandoned the motherland to elope to the Continent in their twenties. Unlike Eveline, they did sail on the boat, but their hearts may have stayed at home—their imaginations certainly did!

Were all of Joyce's writings reflections of early family memory, transformed by the esthetic needs of his genius? Colm Tóibín suggests that "The Dead" reflects much of Joyce's family experiences. He argues that though Joyce himself may never have attended the parties at 15 Usher's Island (the locale of "The Dead"), where his hospitable great-aunts, Mrs. Callanan and Mrs. Lyons, and Mrs. Callanan's daughter Mary Ellen lived, his father, John Stanislaus, certainly had. It was he who carved the goose and made the speech, the way Gabriel Conroy does in "The Dead." Tóibín states: "The figure of Gabriel has elements in common with James Joyce himself as well as his father. Gabriel writes book reviews for the *Daily Express* as Joyce did. His wife is from the west of Ireland, as Nora Barnacle was."

Joyce as Dream Interpreter

Here are his wife Nora's dreams as Ellmann has recounted them.

> At a performance in the theatre
> A newly discovered play by Shakespeare
> Shakespeare is present
> There are two ghosts in the play
> Fear that Lucia may be frightened

And here is Joyce's interpretation: "I am perhaps behind this dream. The 'new discovery' is related to my theory of the ghost in *Hamlet*, and the public sensation is related to a possible publication of that theory or of my own play."

Joyce's theory of the two ghosts in Shakespeare's *Hamlet* is outlined in detail in *Ulysses*, in which Stephen announces his theory about Shakespeare himself playing the role of Hamlet's father, the murdered king, and Hamlet then becoming a ghostly representation of Shakespeare's son Hamnet, who died at the age of eleven. Shakespeare, playing the role of Hamlet's father, would then be talking not only to Prince Hamlet but to the resurrected image of his own son, Hamnet, as well. Is it not strange that Joyce makes no reference in this context to the two ghosts of his own childhood, the dead brother George and the brother who died the year before James was born?

But to return to Joyce's interpretation of Nora's dream: "The figure of Shakespeare present in Elizabethan dress is a suggestion of fame, his certainly (1916 being the tercentenary of his death), mine not so certainly. The fear for Lucia (herself in little) is fear that either subsequent honors or the future development of my mind or art or its extravagant excursions into forbidden territory may bring unrest into her life."

We do not know how Joyce arrived at this interpretation. If Joyce knew his Freud, he would know that after Nora told him the dream, he would have sought Nora's associations to the imagery of the dream, aware of the fact that only the dreamer can interpret the dream by allowing her mind to take each image apart by subjecting it to the free-associative method. The analyst (in this instance Joyce himself) can facilitate the process by pointing out which images the dreamer seems to neglect, seems to favor, et cetera. If Joyce's interpretation has merit, it would seem that he had discussed his theory of the two ghosts in *Hamlet* with his wife and that the conversation between the man and his wife became a day's residue for Nora as she created her dream. Whereas Nora frets about the two ghosts, worrying Lucia, their daughter (who, in reality, became psychotic later), Joyce takes it further by arguing that it is his future development as an artist and his creative excursions into forbidden territory that might unhinge his daughter ("bring unrest into her life"). There is much guilt here and magical thinking as the great author imagines the destructive power of his revolutionary writing.

The interpretation, whether arrived at through paying attention to Nora's associations or not does seem plausible. "I am perhaps behind this dream," Joyce writes (Ellmann, p. 437), and indeed he seems to have been, as this most personal interpretation suggests.

Then Joyce turns to a second dream of his wife.

Lying alone on a hill

A herd of silver cows

A cow speaks, making love

A mountain torrent

Eileen appears

The cow has died of its love

And then Joyce gives his interpretation. "That silver seems to her a fine metal (and not a cheaper form of gold) shows a freedom from conventional ideas, a freedom more strongly shown by the fact that she feels no repulsion at being made love to by a female beast. The cow is warm-bodied, soft skinned and shining for she expects elements of preciousness (Prezioso?) in her woman. The suggestion of the Italian word *vacca* with its connotations of easy morals is in the neighbourhood and possibly, but much more remote, the old poetic name of Ireland 'silk of the Kine.' Here there is no fear of either goring or of pregnancy... Eileen appears as a messenger of those secret tidings which only women bear to women and the silver mountain torrent, a precious and wild element, accompanies the secrecy of her messages with the music of romance. That it has died of love is an old story. Her lovers are all posting to death, death of the flesh, death of youth, death of distance, or of banishment or of a despair lit only by her memory" (Ellmann, p. 437).

Now, what is one to make of such an interpretation? Is this Joyce free associating to the content of the dream as if he had dreamed it himself, or did Nora list her own associations and then Joyce just cited them without attribution? Impossible to know without further data, which Ellmann does not provide. As written, it does sound as if Joyce himself free associated to all of Nora's images as if they were his own. A Freudian psychoanalyst would have waited for Nora's comments, making facilitating interventions of his own only when necessary. "Prezioso" is a reference to an Italian who made sexual overtures to Nora whom Joyce upbraided once he got wind of the matter. One wonders if this is Joyce's jealousy invading the precinct of Nora's dream, or did she actually suggest such a reference to her husband? Or did he wish to possess her dreams as if they were his own in a desperate attempt to possess his wife, such exclusive possession never allowing jealousy to nag him again?

Joyce then cites a third dream of Nora's:

Prezioso weeping
I have passed him in the street
My book *Dubliners* in his hand

Interpretation: "The motive of "Tutto è Sciolto" (from Bellini's *La Sonnambula*) played back to the front. The point with which he tries to wound has been turned against him by her; the motive from which I liberated myself in art he is unable to liberate himself from in life. Again a suffering and aging wooer. His complaint that I pass him (it is to be read the other way round) is a secret disappointment that for her so far it is impossible to unite the friendship of two men through the gift of herself differently to both for that which seemed impossible in the first case is almost impossible in the second case."

This passage, easy to neglect in the torrent of Joyce's associations, is perhaps pivotal for understanding Joyce's psychodynamics. On surface he is suggesting that Nora should be able to "unite the friendship of two men through the gift of herself differently to both for that which seemed impossible in the first case is almost impossible in the second case." Joyce is suggesting that a wife should be able to love two men in a differentiated manner, although that is surely impossible! But is there a far deeper, far more ancient genetic wish being expressed here? Is Joyce not wishing that his mother could have loved his father and James himself, uniting the "friendship of two men through the gift of herself differently to both," and is not this the healthy resolution of the Oedipus complex that development tries to orchestrate no matter the impossibility of the task? Is Joyce attempting to articulate this normal oedipal resolution despite the great difficulty of accomplishing this in such an overcrowded developmental atmosphere? The *resolution* of the Oedipus complex surely depends on an amalgam of developmental compromises. The child's wish to claim one parent and get rid of the other is indeed an impossibility, unless chaos and incest are embraced in an anarchic perverse manner. The only resolution that makes sense developmentally is for the child to establish a détente with the parental authority through a process of identification and repression and postpone his sexual and aggressive intensities until the child becomes an adult, can leave the incestuous home, and build new post-oedipal relationships and a new nonincestuous home. This is the only compromise that can "work" realistically in a mature social contract that does not feel compromised by this developmental finesse and political reality testing that honors the child as a person in her own right and also honors the parents as the authorized caring agents they are. This process works best, obviously, when the parents have resolved their own oedipal conflicts many years ago in childhood: that *memory* of successful, good enough resolution in the past assists parents as they negotiate with an *impossible* child, finding a way to the *possible* by invoking their own struggles in an earlier phase of their own development.

Joyce has fashioned a most complex interpretation out of what Nora has told him. "Prezioso weeping" refers to the journalist Roberto Prezioso who had befriended Joyce years earlier and had once attempted to seduce Nora. Joyce confronted Prezioso, who wept as Joyce upbraided him. It is clear that several years later the man is still on Nora's mind and perhaps even more so on her husband's. Joyce includes the aria "Tutto è Sciolto" from Bellini's *La Sonnambula* as a way of explaining the content of Nora's dream. The opera deals with Elvino's belief that Armina has betrayed him. Armina is a sleepwalker and was once found in the count's bed. "Tutto è Sciolto" translated into English means "All is dissolved or melted," meaning that Elvino believes the betrayal is irreparable. Similarly, Joyce believes that Nora's presumed betrayal can never be completely erased from the unconscious mind of the husband. What is perhaps the most psychoanalytic insight in Joyce's formulation is the idea that the dream content "I have passed him in the street" should be reversed presumably to "He has passed me in the street." There is a psychoanalytic subtlety in this recognition, on Joyce's part, of the dream-work's ability to reverse the order of things in the service of disguise. Similarly, the motive of *La Sonnambula* gets reversed. What Joyce is suggesting is that Nora's would-be lover (Prezioso) would have surpassed Joyce if Nora had succumbed to his advances. Joyce was notoriously jealous throughout his life, an attitude that he often put to fine esthetic purposes in his writings. "Tutto è Sciolto" will appear in the Circe episode in *Ulysses*, and there is also a poem from 1919 entitled "Tutto è Sciolto," and Prezioso's first name, Robert, will be used for the traitorous Robert Hand in Joyce's play *Exiles*! It is clear that the Prezioso reference remained an issue throughout the marriage, clamoring for dream representation at times.

Here is Nora's fourth dream.

    Fully dressed, shitting in her grandmother's garden

    Mary, her sister bids the lover wait

    The lover has a puce face

    His hair in curling papers

    He is bald

    He sits outside a strange house

    A woman no longer young is also there

    The woman puts her leg up

    Her cunt is hairless

    Georgie passes smoking a cigarette

    Anger

    She follows him home

    A quarrel about smoking with Eileen and Stannie

    She screeches with anger

    Her lover expects her to dinner

Ellmann remarks in a footnote: "Joyce offers no interpretation of this dream, but it suggests the transvestism, coprophilia and cuckoldry which pursue at moments the thoughts of Bloom and of his creator."

Let us shift from the examination of Nora's dreams to Joyce's interpretations of his own dreams. The dreams in question cited by Ellmann are from years later, at a time when Joyce was writing *Finnegans Wake*. *The Wake*, as mentioned earlier, was to be Joyce's night book. "The night required and justified a special language," as Ellmann puts it (p. 546), and Joyce was going to create it. "Je suis au bout de l'anglais," Joyce said. He had put the English language to sleep, and in writing of the night, he felt he could not use words in their ordinary connections. It was a radical technique: he would make many of the words multilingual puns and he would attempt to raid the orchards of the dream and come away with the secrets of the night. Ellmann cites what Joyce said to Edmond Jaloux: the novel would be written "to suit the esthetic of the dream, where the forms prolong and multiply themselves, where the visions pass from the trivial to the apocalyptic, where the brain uses the roots of vocables to make others from them which will be capable of naming its phantasms, its allegories, its allusions." This is a beautiful description of what Joyce meant by the esthetic of the dream. It describes, in a more poetic way, what Freud would call the agency of the dream-work as it uses condensation, displacement, symbolism, and the transformation of words into the multiple images of dreams to totally disguise the urgencies of latent content in the profound obfuscations of the manifest content of a dream.

Ellmann says that Joyce astonished his friends by the minuteness of his interest in dream phenomena. Joyce asked his friend William Bird if he ever dreamed that he was reading, and at what speed did he think he was reading in his dreams? When Bird responded that he seemed to read slowly and with difficulty, Joyce's theory was that actually we are talking in our sleep, and since we cannot talk as fast as we read, our dream invents a reason for the slowness. This is pretty daring and intuitive, as Joyce penetrates dream mysteries with great originality and flair. Joyce also had a theory about noises in dreams. He believed that in sleep our senses are dormant except the sense of hearing, which is always awake since one cannot close the ears. "Any sound that comes to our ears during sleep is turned into a dream" (Ellmann, p. 547). Here again Joyce is thinking deeply about the unconscious origins of the dream. He is scientist and artist all in one. Another friend, Myron Nutting, a devotee of psychoanalysis at the time, was amazed at Joyce's shrewdness when he interpreted his dreams. "Mrs. Nutting preserved one of Joyce's dreams and the interpretation he put upon it" (Ellmann, p. 547). Here, then, is Joyce's dream. We have seen how he interpreted Nora's dreams; now we can examine how he interpreted his own.

> I had a curious dream about the Russian ballet. I dreamed that there was a pavilion with sixteen rooms, four on each floor. Someone had committed a crime, and he entered the lowest floor. The door opened on a flower garden. He hoped to get through but when he arrived at the threshold a drop of blood fell on it. I could know how desperate he felt, for he went from the first floor all the way up to the fourth, his hope being that at each threshold his wound was not capable of letting fall another drop. But always it came, an official discovered it, and punctually at the sixteen rooms the drop fell. There were two officials in brocaded silk robes, and a man with a scimitar, who watched him.

Then Joyce asks, as if talking to an invisible dream interpreter: "Can you psychoanalyze it? I will. The rooms represented the twelve signs of the zodiac. Three rooms are the Trinity. The man who had committed the crime is evidently myself. The drop of blood left on each threshold were [*sic*] five franc notes which I borrowed from Wyndham Lewis (with whom Joyce had spent the previous evening). The man with the scimitar represents my wife next morning. The pavilion with light blue lattices was like a box."

Ellmann comments: "The interpretation is a heady mixture of Freud and *The Arabian Nights*" (to which I would add Edgar Allen Poe!). How Freudian is Joyce's interpretation of his dream? When Joyce proclaims that the rooms represented the twelve signs of the zodiac, he seems to be mistaking the number sixteen with twelve, since there were sixteen rooms in the pavilion rather than twelve. He gives no reason for this parapraxis if indeed it is an error. An analyst hearing Joyce recount this dream might bring the parapraxis to his attention. (Could Joyce's confusion of sixteen and twelve have anything to do with the number of people living in his family home at one time? Twelve can become sixteen if we add the parents and Dante Conway (the governess) and John Joyce's uncle William O'Connell, all of whom lived with the family at one point.) If we let imaginative speculation run off with itself, an analyst might say to his patient, "You were one of twelve children, ten living and two who died," and then wait to see what Joyce would make of that. Joyce in his commentary on the dream says, "The man who had committed the crime is evidently myself." Joyce goes on to suggest, as stated earlier, that "the drop of blood left on each threshold were five franc notes which I borrowed from Wyndham Lewis" (with whom Joyce had spent the previous evening). Is Joyce suggesting that the crime was the borrowing of money from a friend? Now Joyce's borrowing from friends was legendary, as if some impoverished part of him felt entitled to the largesse of others. It is unlikely that *Ulysses* or *Finnegans Wake* could have been published at all without the patronage that supported their author throughout the years of their execution. But has Joyce copped a lesser plea here by admitting his guilt for taking from Lewis rather than the deeper, darker, unconscious crime of spilling the blood of his too-numerous siblings? Joyce once remarked that he had twenty-three sisters, alluding to the sibling issue with sarcastic humor. And what is one to make of Joyce's inclusion of the Trinity in his list of associations. Did the crime at its core involve three people, mother, father, and son, an oedipal trinity even more unconsciously entrenched perhaps than the religious one? The religious Trinity is not without its significance, perhaps, as it deals with the father, the son, and the Holy Ghost. Is there a ghost here that Joyce is in flight from, as suggested earlier?

Ellmann proceeds to describe another set of surviving dreams written by Joyce partly before and partly after *Ulysses* was written. They were in a French translation by André du Bouchet, One refers to Joyce signing himself "Ulysses," which he denies. Then another dream, which Joyce wrote out for his friend Gorman, is described in more detail. It deals with Ulysses also in a most arresting manner:

> I saw Molly Bloom on a hillock under a sky full of moonlit clouds rushing overhead. She had just picked up from the grass a child's black coffin and flung it after the figure of a man passing down a side road by the field she was in. It struck his shoulders, and she said, "I've done with you." The man was Bloom seen from behind. There was a shout of laughter from some American journalists in the road opposite, led by Ezra Pound. I was very indignant and vaulted over a gate into the field and strode up to her and delivered the one speech of my life. It was very long, eloquent, and full of passion, explaining all the last episode of *Ulysses* to her. She wore a black opera cloak, or *sortie de bal,* which had become slightly grey and looked like la Duse. She smiled when I ended on an astronomical climax, and then, bending, picked up a tiny snuffbox, in the form of a little black coffin, and tossed it towards me, saying, "And I have done with you, too, Mr. Joyce." I had a snuffbox like the one she tossed me when I was at Clongowes Wood College. It was given to me by my godfather, Philip McCann, together with a larger one to fill it from."

Joyce told a different version of this dream to John Sullivan: "Molly Bloom came calling on me and said, 'What are you meddling with my old business for?'"

She had a coffin in her hand and said, "If you don't change, this is for you" (Ellmann, p. 549 footnote).

Ellmann comments: "This dream resulted in a parody which suggests how Molly was fusing into the character of Anna Livia Plurabelle, heroine of *Finnegans Wake*." This can be detected in the first two lines of the parody:

Man dear, did you ever hear of buxom Molly Bloom at all
As plump an Irish beauty, sir, as any Annie Levy Blumenthal.

Annie Levy Blumenthal was a reference to Anna Livia Plurabelle (one of the central characters in *The Wake*) no doubt. The parody can be thought of as an association to the dream. The parody refers humorously to Joyce's rampant jealousy, which he makes esthetic use of throughout his creations from "The Dead" to *Ulysses* to *Finnegans Wake*. The parody continues:

And she said I'd be her first and last while the wine I poured went bubbling free
Now every male she meets with has a finger in her pie.

This parody is set to the rollicking tune of the old Irish song "Molly Brannigan." Joyce makes fun of his own fears depicting Molly's sexual waywardness in a culinary metaphor!

A parody, written as a reaction to a dream, can be thought of as an association to the dream. Similarly, a poem, written immediately after a dream, can be shown to be a complex association to the dream (Mahon, 2007). We do not have Joyce's interpretation accompanying the dream, but the parody is perhaps a kind of interpretation. The dream and parody taken together would seem to represent a primal conflict between man and woman. Molly Bloom attacks Leopold Bloom in a field, picking up a child's black coffin and throwing it at him, striking him in the shoulders. Joyce (the dreamer) was indignant, vaults over a gate into the field, strides up to Molly, and delivers "the one speech of my life. It was very long, eloquent and full of passion, explaining all the last episode of *Ulysses* to her." She is wearing a black opera cloak and looks like la Duse. She picks up a tiny snuffbox, in the form of a little black coffin, tosses it toward Joyce, saying, "And I have done with you too, Mr. Joyce." Molly is not only done with Bloom but with his creator as well! Joyce makes a most significant comment comparing the snuffbox Molly threw at him to the one that was given to him on his entrance to Clongowes Wood College by his godfather, Philip McCann, "together with a larger one to fill it from." (The concept of a large snuffbox that "feeds" the littler one with its contents has a poignant metaphor embedded in it of a child's wish to be fed by the larger vessels, surely a reference to parents who might be feeding him rather than sending him away.)

What is one to make of this dream's intriguing manifest content, with only Joyce's parody written as an association to the dream to guide us? The dream would seem to confuse the actual snuffbox given to him by his godfather and an aggressive dream gesture, which confuses fiction, fantasy, dream, and the reality of a childhood memory. That confusion, however, may guide us to the latent content even if it does not explicate it. The manifest content depicts a fictitious creation of the author (Molly Bloom) dismissing her fictitious husband (Leopold Bloom) and then dismissing the author himself (James Joyce). This extraordinary manifest drama must have a genetic correlative. Can we assume that Joyce, on being sent away to a boarding school at age six, harbored some resentment toward the parents who must have assumed he was ready for such a separation from his siblings and parents? Might he have felt, at least unconsciously, that his parents were "done with him" and in an act of spiteful retaliation that he was "done with them too." (I am reminded of an analysand whose parents abandoned her at age six as they fled to Europe for a cure for the mother's cancer. When they returned, the child was afraid to express her anger lest they would retaliate and sail away again. A year later, when the mother actually died, the child's defensive reaction was "good riddance," consoling herself with the idea that now she would have her father all to herself. The father's grief was then experienced as a rejection of his daughter's declaration of love for him. The "good riddance" attitude was, of course, a defensive strategy that concealed or tried to conceal the great emotional attachment to the mother that would overwhelm the child if she had experienced it without a defensive disavowal of her great loss. That attitude continued to color the defensive strategies of this woman way into adulthood, whereby she tried to deaden any personal contact with her analyst. By never fully attaching, she could never experience loss, since she had delinked herself, as Bion would characterize it, from objects as a way of never being dependent on them. This kind of trauma plays havoc with the ideal developmental climate in which a child can express hatred of her parents not only with impunity but with the sense that parents can survive the aggression and even love the spunky child for it. This kind of emotional response to parental neglect would be extremely terrifying for a young child to retain conscious knowledge of. The unconscious may well be the only safe receptacle (container) for such anarchic ideas and affects, requiring an act of repression to keep the wolves of aggression at bay. But the repressed will have a lifelong need to represent itself somehow, plead its case in a safe forum. A work of literature may be the ideal repository for such thoughts, requiring an act of sublimation to execute the esthetic plan. Chaucerian Molly Bloom, like the Wife of Bath before her, has all the exorbitant, combustible energy of Joyce himself and surely must be the avatar of so much of his unconscious yearnings. In the manifest content of the dream, he leaps over a gate to deliver a speech of protest against this larger-than-life woman who dares to fire her husband and her creator in one fell swoop. Could this be Joyce himself firing his father and his creator (mother) not unlike the way Molly Bloom fires Bloom and his creator in the manifest content of his dream? A "child's black coffin" is an extraordinary missile to hurl at somebody even in a work of art. What could Joyce be trying to communicate unconsciously? It is hard not to think of this arresting metaphor as a most aggressive communication, a death wish of astonishing communicative power. And surely, the fact that it is a *child's* coffin, has a profound significance, as if the dreamer is drawing special attention to childhood "the nightmare that the world is only beginning to awaken from" (to change Joyce's statement in *Ulysses* a little). It is striking that Joyce leaps over a gate to express his outrage at the sight of a child's coffin being thrown at one of his literary creations. In that sense both a woman and a man express aggression toward each other, Joyce's way of underlining not only the boy's anger at his mother but the boy's fear of the mother's retaliation were he to criticize her. (The black coffin may surely be a reference to the death of the firstborn child that preceded Joyce's own birth, of course.)

Joyce's entry into Clongowes Wood College at the age of six may well be the navel of this dream, a memory clamoring for attention throughout a lifetime. His godfather's gift to the child seems strange now that snuff has all but vanished from the world as a recreational activity. If the memory is real, a six-year-old is being given two snuffboxes, the larger meant as a supplier of the smaller one. Snuff was hailed as medicinal at one point in history. Was a six-year-old supposed to use snuff to soothe himself when he was lonely or angry, or was this meant only as a ceremonial gesture, an adult offering a gift to a child, appealing to some grown-up, precocity in the child as a way of dealing with the reality of the child's complex emotional mental state? Is Joyce revisiting this poignant memory in a dream about a woman's aggression toward two men, one a literary fictional entity, the other the living author and creator of the fictional character? It is interesting to observe that when Joyce himself expresses his anger in the dream, he relies on speech alone to accomplish his goal, delivering "the one speech of my life," whereas Molly accompanies her words with the

210

most aggressive gestures, tossing black coffins at her foes! Of course, in a Freudian analysis of the dream, we argue that the dreamer, Joyce himself, can represent his unconscious wishes through any character he choosessince the dream is his unconscious fiction from start to finish. He can even disguise himself as Ezra Pound and the American journalists laughing at Molly's antics. It is easier to imagine fictional characters dismissing each other and their author than it is to imagine the dismissal of one's own, nonfictional parents in an act of aggression that a child does not feel safe expressing, leaving it to the adult Joyce to find a safe literary expression of his grief and hatred many years later. Could the vision of Molly with every male she meets having "a finger in her pie" be Joyce's way of expressing anger at the mother whose sexuality produced eleven other sibling rivals for the maternal love Joyce must have craved exclusively for himself? Did he wish death not only on the two siblings who actually died but on the nine others who survived, not to mention the oedipal father rounding out the number to ten? Returning to the previous dream for a moment, do the twelve signs of the zodiac, each representing a different birth month, not bring to mind the birth dates of all these siblings Joyce must have wished dead in some repressed part of his psyche?

I have been suggesting that the infantile wishes at the core of Joyce's dreams may have been an elemental fury at both parents for not providing him with the exclusive kind of emotional nourishment he craved not only as a child but throughout his life. At the end of the dream with the sixteen rooms and the drops of blood falling on each threshold, Joyce writes, "There were two officials in brocaded silk robes, and a man with a scimitar who watches him." Joyce then identifies the man with the scimitar as Nora. Does this uncanny trinity presiding over the dream as it comes to an end represent the fierce conscience of the dream brocaded with silk but brandishing a scimitar to enact whatever verdict is reached at the sentencing of the dreaming blood spiller? And why does a man with a scimitar bring his wife to the dreamer's mind? Is this a representation of the phallic woman, equipped with the penis (scimitar) that masculine fear of castration endows her with as a way of denying castration and illustrating it all at once (Bak, 1968). Joyce's dreams are rich and complex in their manifest content and the starkness of the latent infantile wishes that must have spawned the richness of the manifest images is not possible to conjure without Joyce's own associations to his oneiric products, and therefore we are left with speculations, which can only be presented with humility. The speculations are informed by Freudian principles of dream analysis to be sure and are therefore not completely wild or scattershot but still can only be presented as texts that have been stimulated by other texts, and it is in that contextual spirit that I have aired these comments on the dreams of an exceptional writer whose *Ulysses* has been considered as one of the pillars of modernism and perhaps the greatest novel of the twentieth century.

The analysis of the two dreams, to be complete, would have to be informed by Joyce's free associations to every image in each dream. Without this, one is shooting in the dark. One tries to get "associations" to the missing free associations of the dreamer by studying biographies of Joyce and by studying the body of Joycean texts, hoping to find some allusions that would connect with the images in the dreams. I have suggested that the sixteen rooms and Joyce's association connecting sixteen rooms to the twelve signs of the zodiac could be a reference to his many siblings, those who lived and those who died. Could sixteen also be a reference to George's death? He died at age fifteen, in his *sixteenth* year? Could sixteen also be a reference to June 16, 1904, the celebrated day he met Nora Barnacle?

These biographical and literary references, while fascinating and instructive, are not the same as knowing the actual free associations Joyce had when he was reviewing his dreams. Did Joyce know that only by following the free associations doggedly could one arrive at the latent dream thoughts that the dream-work's artistry had transformed into manifest content so expertly? Perhaps he did, but perhaps he also believed that the "esthetic of the dream," as he put it, held artistic potential, which he could exploit so masterfully in *Finnegans Wake*, and that it was that artistic exploitation that intrigued him even more than an accurate Freudian interpretation of his dreams. As noted earlier, Joyce describes the "esthetic of the dream" as though he were putting Freud's primary processes into his own artistic words, and I would like to give Joyce the last words by citing them again:

Joyce, in poetic language, states that *Finnegans Wake* would be written "to suit the esthetic of the dream, where the forms prolong and multiply themselves, where the visions pass from the trivial to the apocalyptic, where the brain uses the roots of vocables to make others from them which will be capable of naming its phantasms, its allegories, its allusions."

EPILOGUE

James Joyce spent seventeen of his final years writing *Finnegans Wake*. He wanted to write a final work of art that would use the esthetic of the dream to capture the unique state humankind spends a third of its life suspended in. He believed that that state needed a new language to depict it, and he set about writing a text full of puns and a mélange of languages to simulate the sleeping state and its dreams. It was as if Joyce believed the dream-work was a most artistic craftsman and that by identifying with this unconscious esthetic force he could create a text that would mimic sleep and the dream state. The jury is still out as to how successful he was from an esthetic point of view. The work has been ridiculed and idealized, with great writers like D. H. Lawrence and Nabokov voicing negative, even nasty commentaries, while Harold Bloom, Edmund Wilson, and Anthony Burgess idealize the achievement, seeing it is part of the Western canon.

I have tried to capture that uncanny world of dreams by examining the artistry of the dream-work and how it can even co-opt the uncanny itself and use it as surreal dream content as it tries to proclaim the innocence of the manifest content by translating and transforming the anything-but-innocent latent dream content into a totally disguised version of itself.

By examining a multiplicity of unusual dream contents, I argue that the dream-work can act as if it has exposed the unconscious mind itself, making its secrets conscious as a way of deceiving the dreamer into thinking the *manifest* has the *latent* in its grasp already and that there is need therefore to dig deeper. If parapraxes, puns, dreams, jokes, the uncanny have already exposed themselves in manifest content, why go any further than that? It is a rare magician who pretends to expose his tricks the better to keep the audience off the scent of all that the magician is not revealing. In that sense this book is written in awe of the dream-work and its artful ingenuities. It is difficult not to talk about it in this personified manner since the extraordinary sense that there is a brilliant unconscious artist at work throughout the sleeping state seems uncanny. The idea that the unconscious never sleeps seems magical: the idea that our mind is indeed under the control of an unconscious artful agency is a blow to the narcissistic certainty that surely consciousness is always in control. Who but a madman would believe that dreams are shaped beyond the reach of consciousness, and yet sanity must accept that there is an agency beyond consciousness that dictates the terms of dreams, its manifest rememberable portion and its latent hidden portion. To Shakespeare's list "the lunatic, the lover and the poet are of imagination all compact," the dreamer should perhaps be added since the glory of unconscious dream artistry is a triumph of unconscious imagination in its own right.

I want to return to a question raised earlier about the exceptional status of the dream in psychoanalysis. Greenson makes it clear that he believes the dream has an exceptional status and that the analysis of the dream is the royal road for getting the genetic past and the current reality to converse with each other free-associatively to further the analytic process in a way no other approach can. He demonstrates his argument with very convincing case material. The analysis of the surrey/buggy/baby carriage made it possible to unearth Mr. M.'s repressed hatred and jealousy about

216

the mother's pregnancies, which seemed like betrayals of his trust. Greenson believes that Mr. M's dream was exceptional as it afforded the analyst the creative opening to the genetic past that was at the core of the neurosis. The analyst's evenly hovering attention to all that Mr. M's free associations had brought to the analytic process to date allowed him to sense that if he changed the word "surrey" to "buggy," this sly genetic interpretation would open the doors of the unconscious wider than ever. The analyst was correct, and the result was most impressive. Does that prove that the dream had an exceptional status in the dynamic analytic process, advancing it like no other communication could have? One imagines that some analysts would say yes and some would say no. But perhaps such disagreements about what is exceptional and what is merely free-associative process, doggedly pursuing the repressed in its piecemeal fashion, are foolish. Might it not be better to suggest that all aspects of the analytic work may seem exceptional at any given moment, any given hour, depending on what affects, dreams, symptoms, character traits, elements of transference or countertransference have come under the free-associative spotlight?

The exceptional status and significance of the dream in furthering analytic process was certainly the conviction of Freud and the early analysts. And Greenson would seem to echo their convictions about the uniqueness of the dream in psychoanalytic process. He quotes Freud's 1933 statement: "Whenever I began to have doubts of the correctness of my wavering conclusions, the successful transformation of a senseless and muddled dream into a logical and intelligible mental process in the dreamer would renew my confidence of being on the right track." My sense is that many analysts have felt that way at times during the analytic process, as a dream is being shredded and all the shreds lead to remarkable insights. Of course, Freud said something similar about an interpretation of the transference: when it illuminates a repressed genetic attitude that has suddenly invaded the current reality of the analytic process, the conviction it brings about the past's ability to corrupt current reality can be a staggering new insight for the analysand! And the current emphasis on the insights that flow from an illuminating recognition of a countertransferential blind spot may seem as exceptional as the dream in the furthering of the dynamic process of analysis. Surely all these emphases have their unique status in complex analytic processes that at times may seem as baffling as the most complicated dream content. This book has emphasized the uniqueness of dreams and their infinite varieties. It suggests that dreams are "a" unique royal road to the unconscious but not "the" only royal road perhaps (Fisher, 2021). As a final statement, I would like to suggest that the more royal roads we can discover, the better our approach will be to the often impregnable citadel of the unconscious.

REFERENCES

Bak, R.C. (1968). "The Phallic Woman." *The Psychoanalytic Study of the Child* 23(1) 15–36. https://doi.org/10.1080/00797308.1968.11822947.

Baudelaire, C. (2008). *The Flowers of Evil.* Translated by James McGowan. Oxford: Oxford University Press.

Battin, D. & Mahon, E. (2003): "Symptom, Screen Memory, and Dream." *The Psychoanalytic Study of the Child* 58(1):246–66. https://doi.org/10.1080/00797308.2003.11800722.

Eastman, A.M. (1975). "London" from *Songs of Experience.* Poem. In *The Norton Anthology of Poetry.* New York: Norton.

Bloom, H. (1975). *The Anxiety of Influence: A Theory of Poetry.* London: Oxford University Press.

——— (1999). *Shakespeare: The Invention of the Human.* New York: Riverhead Books.

Brenner, C. (1992). *The Mind in Conflict* Madison, CT: International Universities Press.

Bronowski, J., & Ariotti, P.E. & Bronowski. R. (1979). *The Visionary Eye: Essays in the Arts, Literature, and Science.* Cambridge, MA: MIT Press.

Carroll, L. (1946). *Alice in Wonderland and Through the Looking Glass.* Kingsport, TN: Grosset & Dunlap.

Chukovsky, K. (1963). *From Two to Five.* Translated and edited by Miriam Morton. Berkeley, CA: University of California Press.

Costain, T.B. (1998). *The Silver Chalice.* Cutchogue, NY: Buccaneer Books.

Eliot, T.S. (1991). "Four Quartets." *Collected Poems, 1909–1962.* New York: Harcourt, Brace, & Co.

Ellmann, R. (1982). *James Joyce: New and Revised Edition.* New York: Oxford University Press.

Empson, W.S. (1965). *Types of Ambiguity.* New York: New Directions Books.

Fisher, C. (In Press). "Are dreams 'The Royal Road to the Unconscious'? Response to Eugene Mahon 'Dreams Within Dreams." *International Journal of Controversial Ideas* 2(2).

Frank, A. (1969). "The Unrememberable and the Unforgettable." *The Psychoanalytic Study of the Child* 24(1):48–77. https://doi.org/10.1080/00797308.1969.11822686.

Frazer, J.G. (1959). *The New Golden Bough.* New York: Criterion Books.

Freud, S. (1897). Letters 70 and 71. *Standard Edition* 1:261–266.

——— (1899). Screen memories. *Standard Edition* 3:301–322.

——— (1900). "The Interpretation of Dreams," in *The Standard Edition* Vol. 4–5.

——— (1900). *Jokes and Their Relation to the Unconscious. Standard Edition* 8.

——— (1908). Creative writers and daydreaming. *Standard Edition* 9:142–153.

———. (1919). The uncanny. *Standard Edition* 17:217–256.

Frost, R. (1983). "Mending Wall." "Birches." In *The Norton Anthology of Poetry*, edited by Alexander Ward Allison. New York: Norton.

——— (1995). "The Figure a Poem Makes." In *Robert Frost: Collected Poems, Prose, and Plays*, edited by R. Poirier and M. Richardson. New York: Library of America.

Greenson, R.R. (1970): "The Exceptional Position of the Dream in Psychoanalytic Practice." *Psychoanalytic Quarterly* 39(4):519–49. https://doi.org/10.1080/21674086.1970.11926541.

Grinstein, A. (1980). *Sigmund Freud's Dreams*. New York: International Universities Press.

Hegel, G.W.F. (2003). *The Phenomenology of Mind*. Mineola, NY: Dover Publications, Inc.

Joyce, J. (1916). *A Portrait of the Artist as a Young Man*. New York: Viking, 1969.

——— (1922). *Ulysses*. New York: Random House, 1961.

Fletcher, J., & Shakespeare, W. (1634). *The Two Noble Kinsmen*. Edited by Eugene M. Waith. New York: Oxford University Press.

Lustman, S.L. (1962): "Defense, Symptom, and Character." *The Psychoanalytic Study of the Child* 17(1) 216–44. https://doi.org/10.1080/00797308.1962.11822846.

Mahon, E.J. (2002). "A Joke in a Dream: a Note on the Complex Aesthetics of Disguise." *The Psychoanalytic Study of the Child* 57(1):452–457. https://doi.org/10.1080/00797308.2002.11800704.

——— (2005). "A Parapraxis in a Dream." *The Psychoanalytic Quarterly* 74(2): 465–484. https://doi.org/10.1002/j.2167-4086.2005.tb00215.x.

———.(2007). "A Pun in a Dream." *Psychoanalytic Quarterly* 76,(4):1367–1373. https://doi.org/10.1002/j.2167-4086.2007.tb00309.x.

——— (1987)..."Ancient Mariner, Pilot's Boy." *The Psychoanalytic Study of the Child* 42(1):489–509. https://doi.org/10.1080/00797308.1987.11823502.

——— (2002). "Dreams within Dreams." *The Psychoanalytic Study of the Child* 57(1):118–30. https://doi.org/10.1080/00797308.2002.11800688.

——— (1992): "Dreams: A Developmental and Longitudinal Perspective." *The Psychoanalytic Study of the Child* 47(1): 49–65. https://doi.org/10.1080/00797308.1992.11822664.

————— (1991). "The 'Dissolution' of the Oedipus Complex: A Neglected Cognitive Factor." *The Psychoanalytic Quarterly* 60(4):628–634. https://doi.org/10.1080/21674086.1991.11927326.

————— (2000): "Parapraxes in the Plays of William Shakespeare." *The Psychoanalytic Study of the Child* 55(1):335–370. https://doi.org/10.1080/00797308.2000.11822529.

Mannoni, O. (1971). *Freud*. New York: Random House,.

Montaigne, M.de. (2003). *The Complete Works: Essays, Travel Journal, Letters*. Trans. by D.M. Frame. New York: Everyman's Library.

Nietzsche, F.W. (1895). *The Antichrist*. New York, Tribeca Books, 2005.

————— (1924). *The Will to Power*. London: Allen.

O'Brien, W.A. *Novalis, (*1971). *Signs of Revolution*. Durham: Duke University Press.

O'Flaherty, W D. (1984). *Dreams, Illusion and Other Realities*. Chicago: University of Chicago Press.

Opie, I.A. & Opie, P. (1959). *The Lore and Language of Schoolchildren*. Oxford, England: Clarendon Press.

Ovid (8 A.D.). *Metamorphoses*. Trans. by F.J. Miller and G.P. Goold. Cambridge Mass: Harvard University Press, 1984.

Partridge, E. (1958). *Origins: A Short Etymological Dictionary of Modern English*. London: Routledge & Kegan.

Platt, L. (2012). Introduction to Finnegan's Wake by James Joyce. London: Wordsworth Editions Limited.

Proust, M. (1913–1927). In Search of Lost Time. Transl. by M. Treharne. New York: Modern Library, 2003.

Sarnoff, C.A. (1970). "Symbols and Symptoms." *Psychoanalytic Quarterly* 9(4):550–562. https://doi.org/10.1080/21674086.1970.11926542.

Schafer, R. (1968). "The Mechanism of Defense." *The International Journal of Psychoanalysis* 49(1):49–62.

Shakespeare, W. (1596–1599). "The Merchant of Venice." In *The Riverside Shakespeare*, edited by G.B. Evans, 250–85. Boston: Houghton Mifflin Company, 1974.

———— (1599–1601). *Hamlet*. Edited by C. Hoy. New York: Norton, 1992.

———— (1608). *King Lear*. Edited by D.M. Bevington and D.S. Kastan. Toronto: Bantam Books, 2005.

———— (1623). *The Tragedy of Antony and Cleopatra*. Edited by B. Everett. New York: Signet Classic, 1998.

Shengold, L. (2004). "A Brief Psychoanalytic Note on Wordsworth, Poetic Creativity, and Love." *The American Poetry Review* 33(1)27–29. http://www.jstor.org/stable/20682448.

Silber, A..(1983). "A Significant 'Dream within a Dream.'" *Journal of the American Psychoanalytic Association* 31(4):899–915. https://doi.org/10.1177/000306518303100403.

Skeat, W.W. (1910). *An Etymological Dictionary of the English Language*. Oxford: Clarendon Press.

Smith, H.F. (2003). "Common and Uncommon Ground: A Panel Exchange." *Journal of the American Psychoanalytic Association* 51(4):1311–1335. https://doi.org/10.1177/00030651030510042101.

Spitz R.A., & Cobliner, W.G. (1965). *The First Year of Life: A Psychoanalytic Study of Normal and Deviant Development of Object Relations*. New York: International Universities Press,

Stein, M.H. (1981). "The Unobjectionable Part of the Transference." *Journal of the American Psychoanalytic Association* 29(4):869–892. https://doi.org/10.1177/000306518102900405.

Thonemann, P. (2020). *An Ancient Dream Manual. Artemidorus' The Interpretation of Dreams*. Oxford: Oxford University Press.

Untermeyer, L. (1964). *Robert Frost: A Backward Look*. Washington, DC: Library of Congress.

Winnicott, D.W. (1958). "Transitional Objects and Transitional Phenomena: A Study of the First Not-Me Possession." In *Collected Papers*, 229–242. New York: Basic Books.

——— (1971). *Playing and Reality*. New York: Basic Books,

Yazmajian, R.V. (1968). "Slips of the Tongue in Dreams." *Psychoanalytic Quarterly* 37(4):588–595. https://doi.org/10.1080/21674086.1968.11926476.

——— "Slips of the Tongue." *The Psychoanalytic Quarterly* 34, no. 3 (1965): 413–419. https://doi.org/10.1080/21674086.1965.11926356.

Yeats, W.B. (2002). "The Cap and Bells." Poem. In *The Yeats Reader: A Portable Compendium of Poetry, Drama, and Prose*, 26–27. Edited by Richard J. Finneran. New York: Scribner Poetry.

www.ingramcontent.com/pod-product-compliance
Lightning Source LLC
Chambersburg PA
CBHW062127020426
42335CB00013B/1133